Jewish Heroes BOOK TWO

Jewish

Heroes BOOK TWO

by Sadie Rose Weilerstein

Illustrations by Lili Cassel

United Synagogue Commission on
Jewish Education
NEW YORK 5717–1956

1986 printing

Copyright 1956 by The United Synagogue of America

All rights reserved. No part of this book may be reproduced in any form without permission in writing from the publisher except by a reviewer who may quote brief passages in a review to be printed in a magazine or newspaper. Design by Peter Oldenburg. Printed in the United States of America.

TO **Reuben**

Acknowledgment

THE MAKING of a textbook is a cooperative effort. It is for this reason that I wish to express my gratitude to those who helped in the preparation of this book. I wish to thank the members of the United Synagogue Commission on Jewish Education, who planned the series and who took time from their many activities to consider the manuscript and submit oral and written reports. Among these were Rabbi Josiah Derby, the chairman of the Commission and Mr. Henry R. Goldberg, chairman of the Committee on Textbook Publication.

Dr. Abraham E. Millgram served as editor and attended to the countless details attendant on the planning and production of the book. His wide experience in Jewish education and in the preparation of textbooks made his guidance of particular value. I am deeply grateful to him.

Thanks are also due Mr. Peter Oldenburg who designed the book and to the gifted artist, Miss Lili Cassel, whose illustrations illuminate the text.

The readers appointed by the Commission, until now known to me as A, B, C, D, and E, were Mrs. Hillel Henkin, Mrs. Samuel Levine, Mrs. Judith Mandelbaum, Mrs. Theresa K. Silber, and Mrs. Orah Zohar. Their criticisms, based on classroom experience, were most helpful and stimulating. It is my hope that they will find that I profited by them.

I wish also to express my warm appreciation to Dr. Robert Gordis who clarified for me certain moot points; to Mr. Hillel Millgram for his critical reading of the manuscript; to Mrs. Zipporah Olesker whose encouragement in the early stages of the work meant much to me; to my dear friend and most helpful of critics, Miss Emily Solis-Cohen; and to the youngest of my readers and listeners, my nephew Michael Victor and my little friends and neighbors, Virginia Gordon, Andrea Sustin, and Suzanne and David Stogel.

Books were, of course, an indispensable help. I single out, for the special insights which they gave me, *Akiba* by Dr. Louis Finkelstein; Dr. Judah Goldin's section on the Talmud in Volume I of *The Jews, Their History, Culture and Religion* (edited by Dr. Louis Finkelstein); and *A History of the Jews* by Dr. Solomon Grayzel.

Above all I am indebted to my husband. Without his support I doubt whether this book would have been completed. His knowledge of the Hebrew sources was always at my disposal. His unfailing encouragement was my stay.

S. R. W.

Dear Teacher:

You may be interested in a remark of Michael, my eight-year-old "reader," who took his responsibility as critic with great seriousness.

"Aunt Sadie," he said anxiously, "maybe you'd better not depend on me. I'm the right age, but I'm in the highest reading group in my class."

This book is intended primarily for eight- and nine-year-olds. But as Michael was aware, children of the same age group vary in reading ability, in background, in aptitudes. That is why the teacher is so important to the writer.

Because *you* are there, I have felt free to introduce an occasional word that is not found in the vocabulary list for eight-year-olds.

Because *you* are there, I have let the stories and pictures tell themselves, uncluttered by definitions and lengthy explanations. In the hands of a skilled teacher, a word of introduction, a brief discussion called forth by a picture, an object, a question, can give the class the necessary background more naturally and effectively than many pages in the text.

Because of *you*, I am less troubled than I might otherwise be by the rich material which could not be included; prophetic passages that rise from between the lines to rebuke me for their omission; rabbinic stories begging to be told. A textbook is necessarily limited. Out of the wealth of material available, which stories and incidents were we to select? The choice had to be based not only on the appeal of the individual story but on its contribution to the whole, the extent to which it illuminated the character and contributions of the particular hero.

But *you* can enrich the text. Supplementary stories introduced in the course of the review may prove more helpful than if they were incorporated in the text. They will make the child aware that what he is getting is no more than a foretaste of a rich banquet which may be his. Engage his interest and curiosity and he will ask for more.

This is not meant to be a teacher's guide. I wish only to answer a question that has often been put to me.

Is this volume intended to be read by the teacher or the pupils?

By both. It is better, on the whole, to have the initial presentation made by the teacher who is thoroughly familiar with the material and can tell or read the story with understanding and enthusiasm. Under no circumstances should the lesson become a classroom exercise in oral reading. It is most important, however, that the children re-read the stories by themselves, preferably at home with the cooperation of the parents. This should be purposeful reading in preparation for classroom projects, dramatizations of various kinds, games, quizzes, the planning of an assembly program, of a frieze to decorate the room.

For the child who enjoys reading aloud the review period offers opportunities. To cite a few examples: (1) "A Radio Play" in which roles are assigned, the teacher acts as narrator, and the children come in with the dialogue using the direct discourse in the text. (2) "Find the Answer" in which questions are asked and the answers are read directly from the book. (3) "Match the Picture" in which the teacher or a pupil points to a picture in the book and the class hunts for the passage it illustrates. The experienced teacher will think of various other methods to keep her class interested and alert.

The important thing is to make the personalities "come alive." A textbook is no more than a teaching aid. It is my hope that you will find this an effective one.

S. R. W.

Contents

Do You Remember?   15

    PROPHETS

The Story of the Prophet Elijah

    A King, a Queen, and a Prophet   31
    There Shall Be No Rain   34
    The Great Test   36
    The Still Small Voice   42
    Naboth's Vineyard   44
    The Chariot of Fire   46

The Story of Amos

    Amos the Shepherd   51
    Hate Evil and Love Good   54

The Story of Isaiah

    How Isaiah Became a Prophet   58
    Return to Your God   60
    The King Who Had No Faith   64

The Good King Hezekiah	68
God Saves Jerusalem	69
Swords into Plows	72

The Story of Jeremiah

Jeremiah Becomes a Prophet	74
The Burning of the Scroll	78
Jerusalem Is Destroyed	83
God Comforts Jeremiah	87

LEADERS OF THE EXILE AND THE RETURN

The Story of Daniel

Daniel Is Brought to the Palace	92
The Stone That Became a Mountain	96
Nebuchadnezzar Learns a Lesson	99
The Writing on the Wall	103
In the Lion's Den	106

The Story of Ezra and Nehemiah

Ezra, Son of a Scribe	110
God's Torah	114
Ezra Goes Up to Jerusalem	117
Shocking News	118
With Spade and Sword	120

Nehemiah Sees That Justice Is Done	124
The People Learn to Love the Torah	126

The Story of Esther

The Maiden Named Hadassah	130
Esther Becomes Queen	132
Haman Plots Against the Jews	134
Esther Saves Her People	139

The Story of Judah Maccabee

Antiochus the Madman	146
For the Holy Laws	148
Whoever Is for the Lord, Follow Me	151
The Few Against the Many	154
And the Light Did Not Go Out	158

RABBIS AND TEACHERS

The Story of Hillel

On the Schoolhouse Roof	162
A Wager Is Lost	166
Hillel Says—Shammai Says	169
If You Were He	171
Both Speak God's Words	174
The Whole Torah	176

The Story of Johanan ben Zakkai

In the Shadow of the Temple	179
Johanan's Pupils	182
War With Rome	185
Escape in a Coffin	188
The School That Saved a People	193

The Story of Akiba

Akiba and Rachel	198
The Shepherd Becomes a Scholar	202
A Good Wife Is Rewarded	204
Rabbi, Teacher and Judge	207
A Broken Promise	209
Days of Peril	213
His Life for the Torah	215

The Story of Rabbi Judah the Prince

An Exchange of Babies	218
For the Sake of the Torah	220
Judah Becomes Judah the Prince	222
Rabbi Learns From His Pupils	225
No Time to Sleep	227
Soft and Hard Tongues	231
Written Laws and Oral Laws	232
The Making of the Mishnah	235
A Righteous Man's Monument	236

Do You Remember?

Do you remember Abraham who came to know God when all the people around him were worshipping idols? Do you remember how God called him, saying:

Leave your country and your father's house and go to a land that I will show you. I will make of you a great nation. Through you all the peoples of the earth shall be blessed.

Here are pictures to remind you of this story and many others you have read.

The map you just saw shows Abraham's journey from Haran to the Land of Canaan.

Abraham has crossed the wide river and is leading his followers across the hot bare desert. Can you find his wife Sarah? His nephew Lot?

Now the long hard journey is over. The Land of Canaan lies before them—green pastures, mountains, running streams. Abraham's heart is full of joy, for he hears the voice of God saying:

Abraham, I give this good land to you and to your children and your children's children forever.

You have seen this picture before, Abraham welcoming three strangers to his tent. Abraham is always kind to strangers. He does not know that these are special guests, messengers of God. They bring joyful news. Sarah is to bear Abraham a son.

Now at last Abraham has a beloved son, Isaac, to whom he can teach God's way.

What is God's way?

Abraham knows that it is *to do what is right and just.*

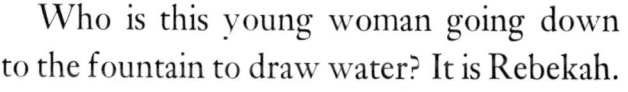

Who is this young woman going down to the fountain to draw water? It is Rebekah.

And the old man beside the kneeling camels, who is he? He is Abraham's servant, Eliezer. Abraham has sent him to Haran to bring back a wife for Isaac.

In a moment Eliezer will run up to Rebekah and ask her for a drink of water and she will give it to him. She will also offer to draw water for his thirsty camels.

Rebekah will be a fitting wife for Isaac.

These twin babies are the sons of Isaac and Rebekah. Which of the two will become the father of the new nation that is to follow in God's way?

It could not be Esau. Esau's dream is to be a mighty hunter. It will be Jacob, the shepherd, whose dream is of a ladder reaching from earth to heaven.

A time will come when God will give Jacob a new name, Israel, Prince of God.

These are the sons of Jacob. From them will come the twelve tribes of Israel.

Do you remember Joseph and his dreams and the coat of many colors his father, Jacob, gave him? Do you remember how his brothers in their anger sold him into Egypt, leading their father to believe that he had been killed by a wild beast? Do you remember how Joseph became a great lord in Egypt and saved many lives in a time of hunger? Among those he saved were his own father and brothers.

This is the road down which Joseph was carried by the merchants to whom his brothers sold him.

Down this road the brothers travelled to buy grain in Egypt that their families might not starve. Thus they learned that Joseph was alive.

Now the aged Jacob is travelling the same road. With his sons and daughters, his grandchildren and great-grandchildren, his flocks and herds, Jacob is going down to Egypt to Joseph his son.

Years and years have passed. The Children of Israel are still in the land of Egypt. But they are no longer free. A new Pharaoh has enslaved them.

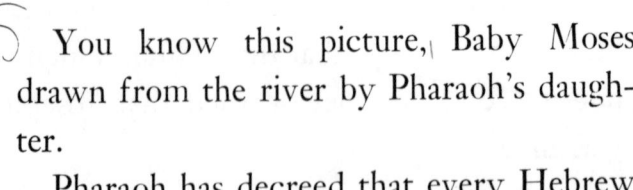

You know this picture, Baby Moses drawn from the river by Pharaoh's daughter.

Pharaoh has decreed that every Hebrew baby boy is to be drowned. Will the princess turn little Moses over to the soldiers? No. Pharaoh's daughter is gentle and kind.

She will adopt Moses and raise him as her own son.

When Moses grows up he will turn in pity to the Hebrew slaves. He will demand of Pharaoh in God's name, "Let my people go."

Moses will lead the Children of Israel out of Egypt, from slavery to freedom.

Do you see Moses coming down the mountain with the Tablets of the Law? This is Mount Sinai where the Children of Israel received the Ten Commandments. They have made a solemn promise: *All that the Lord commands we will do and obey.*

For forty years the Children of Israel wandered in the wilderness. During all these years Moses was their leader and teacher. He taught them to love God and to keep His Commandments. He taught them that God wanted them to love one another, to be merciful and just. Patiently, he tried to make the Children of Israel a holy nation, following God's ways.

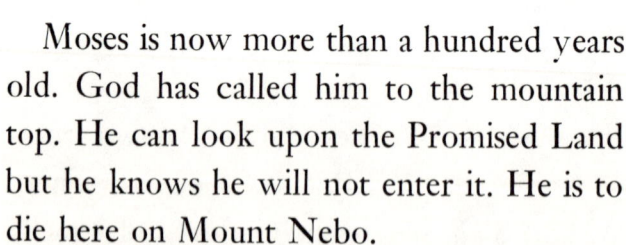

Moses is now more than a hundred years old. God has called him to the mountain top. He can look upon the Promised Land but he knows he will not enter it. He is to die here on Mount Nebo.

Below in the plain, the people are mourning. Nevermore will there be a man like Moses.

Who is leading the children of Israel into the Promised Land?

Joshua.

He will conquer the Land of Canaan and divide it among the tribes.

Now the Children of Israel are farmers in Canaan, the land God promised to their fathers. Are they keeping God's commandments? Are they teaching their neighbors God's ways?

No! The Children of Israel are copying the ways of their neighbors. Do you see them bringing offerings to the altar on the hilltop? It is not an altar to God. It is an altar to Baal whom the Canaanites worship.

When the Children of Israel trusted in God they were strong.

Now they are losing their faith and their courage.

The enemies of Israel are coming up against them. The tribes of Israel are too weak to resist.

But new leaders arise to save them, men and women whose trust is in God.

Deborah

Gideon

Samuel

It was to Samuel the people came, demanding, "Give us a king that we may be like other nations."

This is Saul, the young king Samuel gave them. Do you see how stern Samuel looks? He is reminding the people that Israel is *not* to be like the other nations around them. In Israel *the king together with the people must obey God's commands.*

David the shepherd became the second king of Israel.

It was King David who united the tribes into a strong nation and made Jerusalem the capital.

It was David who wrote the psalms.

David chose Solomon from among his sons to rule after him.

You remember Solomon's dream.

"Ask what you wish and it shall be given you," God said to him. And the young king answered, "Oh, God, give me wisdom that I may rule the people justly."

King Solomon built the Holy Temple in Jerusalem and placed in it the Ark with the *Ten Commandments of God.*

Solomon's son did not pray for wisdom to rule the people justly. He was a foolish young king and took advice from young and foolish companions. Ten of the tribes rebelled and formed a kingdom of their own. The two tribes of the south remained loyal.

You can see on the map what happened. The part colored black is the Kingdom of Judah. The part colored tan is the Kingdom of Israel. The Kingdom of Israel is much larger. It is made up of ten tribes. But the Kingdom of Judah has Jerusalem with the Holy Temple. Now there are *two* kings, *two* capitals, *two* armies in the Land of Israel.

What happened next? The stories in this book will tell you.

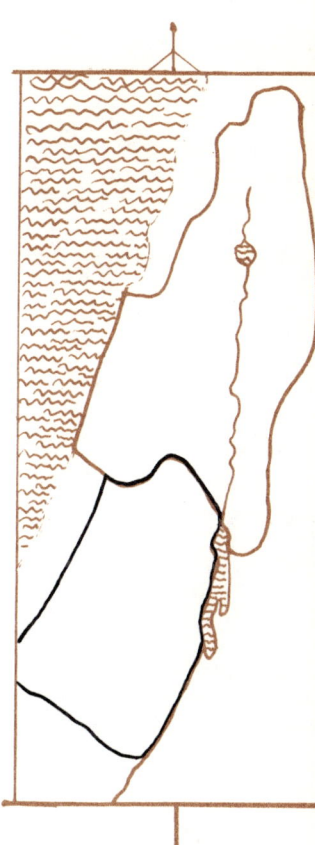

Prophets

ELIJAH

AMOS

ISAIAH

JEREMIAH

The Story of the Prophet Elijah

A King, a Queen, and a Prophet

IN THE LAND of Israel there once lived a king named Ahab. Ahab did more to displease God than any king before him. And his wife was more wicked than he. She was a princess from a neighboring land, a land where people prayed to Baal, not to God. The name of the queen was Jezebel. Whatever she wanted she had always managed to get. Now she wanted all the people of Israel to pray to Baal as she did.

"Build me a beautiful temple in honor of my god Baal," she said to Ahab.

And Ahab, to please his queen, built the temple.

"Come into the temple with me," said Jezebel.

And King Ahab went in and knelt before Baal.

"A temple of Baal must have priests of Baal," said Jezebel.

31

King Ahab let her send to her old home for one thousand priests of Baal. Four hundred and fifty of them ate at the queen's table. Soon there were altars of Baal on every hill top in the land. Sounds of stamping feet, of shouting and wild laughter were heard by the Israelite farmers in the valley. They went up to the altars to see what was happening. Many returned, bringing offerings for Baal.

"We can serve God *and* Baal," they said.

Queen Jezebel was pleased.

"Soon Baal, not the Lord God, will be the god of Israel," she said.

But Jezebel had forgotten about the prophets. The prophets, you remember, were men whom God chose to be his messengers. Up and down the land they went,

teaching people how God wanted them to live. The prophets knew that one could not serve both God and Baal. God wants men to love one another, to do what is just and right. But the ways of Baal's priests were shameless and cruel.

The prophets warned the people of Israel not to go up to Baal's altars.

Enraged, Jezebel sent for her soldiers and commanded them: "Search out and kill every prophet of the Lord. Let not one of them escape."

Hundreds of prophets were killed at this time. Others fled from the land or hid in caves. But there was one prophet who would not keep silent. The name of this prophet was Elijah.

There Shall Be No Rain

King Ahab met Elijah for the first time, soon after the prophets of the Lord had been put to death. He was paying a visit to the captain of his army, when suddenly a stranger stood before him. The man wore the mantle of a prophet, a rough sheepskin cloak. His hair was long, his eyes stern.

"The Lord God of Israel has sent me to you," the stranger said. "As the Lord lives, there shall be no rain nor dew in the land until I give the word."

Before the king could speak, the man was gone. Troubled, King Ahab asked the servants if they knew who the stranger might be.

"It is Elijah," they said. "He is a prophet of the Lord. He lives in Gilead across the Jordan River."

Ahab tried to put the words of Elijah out of his thoughts. But the time of the early rains came and no rain fell. And the time of the second rains came, and still the sky was clear and cloudless. The earth dried up. The grass withered.

Ahab sent out messengers to hunt for Elijah. Up and down the land they went, questioning everyone. Near the Jordan River they heard people talking about the prophet.

One said, "Elijah is hiding in a cave in the mountains of Gilead."

Another said, "The Lord has commanded the birds to feed him. Ravens fly down morning and evening bringing him bread and meat."

So the messengers crossed the Jordan River. They searched in the wild and lonely mountains of Gilead. They searched in the lands beyond the mountains. But they could not find Elijah.

The Great Test

Three years passed, and still there was no rain. King Ahab sent for Obadiah, his head servant.

"Come," the king said, "let us go through the land ourselves, to all the springs and brooks. Perhaps we shall find a little grass—enough to keep alive the mules and horses, and what is left of the cattle."

So the two set out, Ahab going in one direction and Obadiah in the other. Suddenly, Obadiah saw Elijah standing before him.

Now Obadiah was a man who had always served God. In the days when Jezebel was putting the prophets to death, Obadiah had hidden one hundred of them in a cave, and brought them bread and water. So Obadiah bowed to the ground before the prophet.

"Is it you, my lord Elijah?" he cried.

"It is I," Elijah answered. "Go and say to the king, 'Elijah is here.'"

But Obadiah was afraid to tell the king. He said, "When I leave, you will disappear as you did before. If Ahab comes and does not find you, he will surely kill me."

Elijah answered, "As truly as God lives, I will appear before the king today."

So Obadiah hurried to King Ahab with the news. When they returned, they found Elijah waiting for them.

"Is it you, you troubler of Israel?" King Ahab said.

Elijah answered, "*I* have not brought trouble upon Israel, but *you,* for you have turned away from the commandments of God and gone over to Baal."

Then Elijah told Ahab to gather at Mount Carmel all the leaders of Israel, and the four hundred and fifty priests of Baal. King Ahab did not dare to refuse. All the people assembled, the men of Israel on one side, and the priests of Baal on the other side. Between them stood Elijah.

Turning to the men of Israel, Elijah cried, "How long will you hop back and forth between two opinions? If the Lord is God, follow Him. If Baal, follow him."

The people made no answer.

Again Elijah spoke, "I stand alone, the only one left of the prophets of God. But the priests of Baal are four hundred and fifty men. Let us make a test."

Then he turned to the priests of Baal.

"Prepare a young bull for an offering," he said. "Place it on the wood that is on your altar, but put no fire under it. I will do the same. Then call on your gods, and I will call on my God. The one who sends down fire to burn up the offering, is the true God."

All the people answered, "It is a fair test."

The priests of Baal placed their offering on the altar, but put no fire under it, and they called on the name of Baal.

"O, Baal, answer us! O, Baal, answer us!" they cried, dancing around the altar. From morning to noon they called, but there was no answer.

At noon, Elijah mocked them, saying, "Cry louder. Perhaps your god is busy, or has gone hunting, or is on a journey. Perhaps he is asleep and needs to be awakened."

The priests cried louder, and slashed themselves with knives and swords until blood gushed out, for this was their custom. They leaped upon the altar calling, "O, Baal, answer us!"

So the hours passed. Evening was coming on. And still there was no answer to their prayers.

Then Elijah said to the men of Israel, "Come near me."

When they drew near, he took twelve stones, one for each of the tribes of Israel, and repaired the altar of God that had been broken down. Around the altar he dug a trench. Then he took the offering and laid it on the wood upon the altar.

"Fill four jars with water," he said to the people. "Pour it on the offering and on the wood."

When they had done this, he said, "Do it a second time."

And they did it a second time and a third, until the water ran down from the altar and filled the trench.

Then Elijah prayed, "O, Lord God of Abraham, of Isaac, and of Israel, let the people know this day that You are God. Answer me, O God, answer me, that the hearts of the people may turn back to You."

As he spoke, fire from heaven came down upon the altar. It burned up the offering and the wood, the stones and the dust. It licked up the water in the trench.

The people saw it and bowed to the ground, crying, "The Lord, He is God. The Lord, He is God."

Then Elijah went up to the mountain top, taking his young servant with him.

"Go and look toward the sea," he said to the servant.

While the lad was gone, he bowed his head between his knees and prayed.

The servant returned, saying, "I see nothing there."

"Look again," Elijah said.

Seven times he sent the servant back.

The seventh time the boy said, "A cloud as small as a man's hand is rising out of the sea."

Then Elijah said, "Go. Say to King Ahab, 'Get into your chariot and hurry home, or the rain will stop you.'" So the boy ran ahead and Elijah followed.

The small cloud had spread until it covered the heavens.

Ahab mounted his chariot and set out across the plains. And Elijah ran before him all the way to the gates of the city. As he ran, rain came pouring down.

When Jezebel learned what had happened to her priests, her eyes grew hard with anger. She arose and sent a message to Elijah. "As surely as you are Elijah and I am Jezebel, you shall be a dead man tomorrow at this time."

Elijah fled for his life.

The Still Small Voice

Elijah fled southward, to the land of Judah. In the wilderness, he sat down to rest under a tree.

"O, God," he prayed, "I can bear no more. Pray, let me die."

Then, weak with hunger and thirst, for he had taken with him neither food nor water, he lay down under the tree and fell asleep.

Suddenly, he felt someone touch him. A voice said, "Arise! Eat!"

Elijah opened his eyes. Near his head was a cake baked on hot stones, and a jar of water. He arose and ate and drank. Strengthened by the food and water, Elijah traveled through the wilderness for forty days and nights until he came to Mount Horeb, the mountain where Moses had once heard the voice of God. There, in a cave, Elijah waited to see if God would speak to him.

Suddenly a mighty wind passed by. It tore at the mountains and broke the rocks in pieces. But the Lord was not in the wind. After the wind came an earthquake, but the Lord was not in the earthquake. After the earthquake came a fire, but the Lord was not in the fire. After the fire came a still small voice. As soon as Elijah heard it, he covered his face with his mantle. Then he went out and stood in the entrance of the cave.

"What are you doing here, Elijah?" the voice asked gently.

Elijah answered, "The people of Israel have turned away from You, O Lord. They have thrown down Your altars and killed Your prophets. I, I alone am left, and they are seeking to take my life."

Then the voice said, "You are not alone, Elijah. There are still seven thousand men in Israel who have not bowed down to Baal. Go back the way you came."

Then God told Elijah what he was next to do.

Elijah arose and set out once more for Israel.

Naboth's Vineyard

King Ahab stood in the beautiful garden of his palace, talking to a man of Israel named Naboth. Naboth owned a vineyard nearby where he tended his vines as his father and his grandfather had done before him. Now, King Ahab had many vineyards of his own, but he had set his heart on this one that belonged to Naboth. It was close to the palace and he wanted it for a garden of herbs.

So he said to Naboth, "Give me your vineyard and I will pay you for it, or will give you a better vineyard in its place."

But in those days it was considered wrong for a man to sell land which had come down in his family. A father kept his vineyard and his fields so that his sons and grandsons might have them after him.

So Naboth said to King Ahab, "God forbid that I should give up this vineyard which came to me from my fathers."

Ahab went back to the palace, disappointed and sulking, and lay down on his bed. His servants brought him food, but he turned his head away and refused to eat.

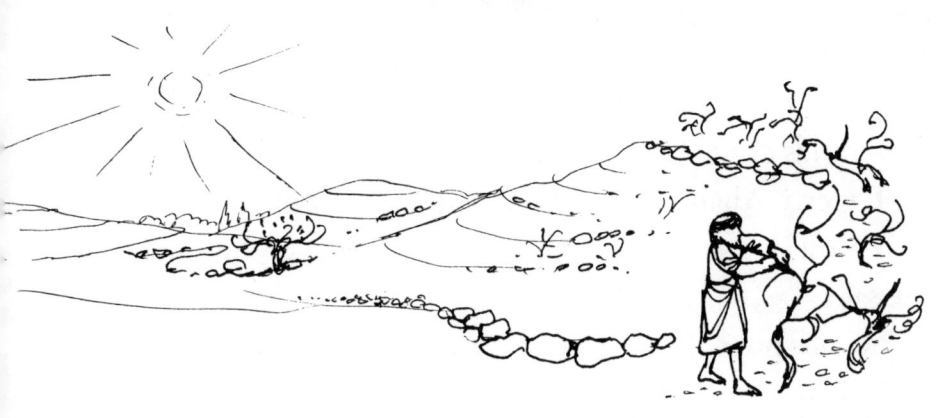

Then Jezebel, his wife, came to him.

"Why are you so disturbed that you eat no food?" she asked.

Ahab answered, "It is because of Naboth." And he told Jezebel what had happened.

Jezebel said scornfully, "Are you not king in Israel? Arise, eat, and let your heart be merry. I will give you Naboth's vineyard."

But this was not so easy as Jezebel had thought. In other lands a king could do whatever he pleased, but in Israel even the king had to obey the law. Jezebel waited for a fast day when all the people were gathered together. Then she got two wicked men to go before the judges and swear, "We heard Naboth curse God and the king."

It was a lie, but the people did not know it.

The judges said, "Naboth must die. Two men have sworn that he cursed God and the king."

So innocent Naboth was put to death.

Then Jezebel hurried to Ahab and said, "The vineyard which Naboth refused to sell you is now yours, for Naboth is dead. Go and take it."

Eagerly Ahab arose and hurried down to the vineyard.

"Now I can pull up the vines and plant my garden," he said.

As he spoke, he heard a voice behind him.

"Have you killed Naboth and also taken his vineyard?"

Ahab turned quickly, for he knew the voice.

"Have you found me, O my enemy?" he cried.

Elijah answered, "God has sent me to say to you, 'All your life you have done what was evil. Now the evil that you brought upon others shall come upon you!' "

Then Elijah told Ahab of dreadful things that were to happen to him in the days to come. Ahab realized at last how great was his wickedness. He hurried out of the vineyard and put on sackcloth, and fasted, and went about quietly in order that God might see that he was sorry for his evil deeds.

But in Jezebel there was no change at all.

The Chariot of Fire

Elijah lived long enough to see the prophets of God return to Israel. By the time he was an old man there were companies of them in the cities of Beth El and Jericho. The young men, who were their followers, called themselves "Sons of the Prophets."

Elijah, too, had a young follower who was like a son to him. His name was Elisha. People liked to tell the story of their first meeting.

Elisha's father was a farmer who owned broad fields near the Jordan River. It took twelve men with twelve yoke of oxen to plow his land. One day Elisha and his father's servants were plowing behind the oxen, when suddenly Elijah appeared. Without speaking, Elijah crossed the field, threw his mantle over Elisha and went on. Elisha knew this was a sign that God had chosen him to become a prophet. He left his oxen and ran after Elijah.

"Let me kiss my mother and father good-bye," he said. "Then I will follow you."

"Go," Elijah said.

So Elisha bade his family and his friends good-bye. Then he followed after Elijah to serve him, and to learn his ways. Since that time Elisha had never left Elijah.

Elijah was by now a very old man. One day he said to Elisha, "My son, stay here, I beg you, for God has sent me to Beth El."

Elisha answered, "As surely as the Lord lives, and as you live, I will not leave you."

So they went to Beth El together. The Sons of the Prophets came out to Elisha and said to him, "Do you know that God is going to take your master away from you today?"

Elisha answered. "Yes, I know it. Do not speak of it."

Again Elijah said, "I beg you, stay here, Elisha, for the Lord has told me to go to Jericho."

But Elisha said, "As the Lord lives, and as you live, I will not leave you."

So they went on to Jericho. At Jericho, also, the Sons of the Prophets said to Elisha, "Do you know that God is going to take your master away from you today?"

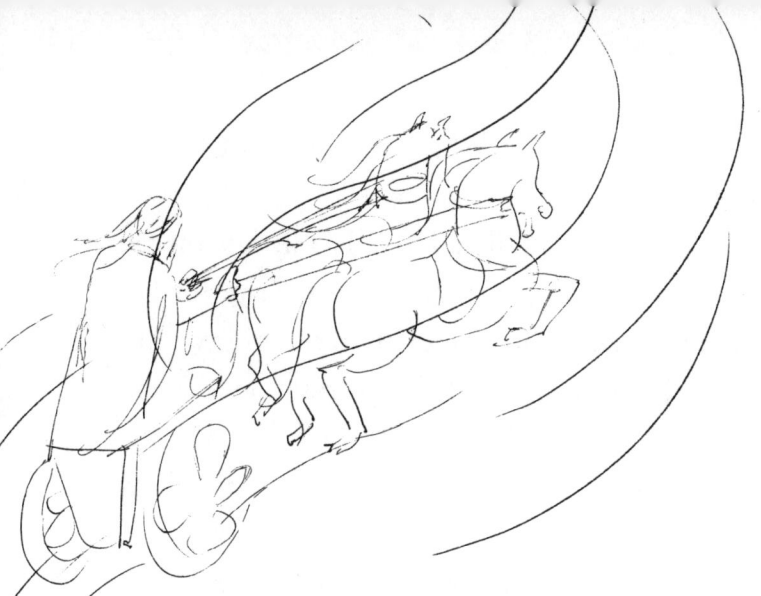

"Yes, I know it," Elisha answered. "Do not speak of it."

A third time Elijah said, "Elisha, remain here, I beg you, for God has sent me to the Jordan River."

But Elisha would not leave his master and they crossed the Jordan River together.

Then Elijah said, "Ask what you want me to do for you before I am taken away."

Elisha answered, "My master, I want only to be like you. Let me have a double measure of your spirit."

"You have asked a hard thing," Elijah said. "Nevertheless, if you see me when I am taken away from you, it will be a sign that you shall have your wish."

A storm arose as they were talking. The wind blew and lightening flashed. Suddenly, a chariot of fire and horses of fire came down between them. Before Elisha's eyes, Elijah went up to heaven in a whirlwind.

"My father, my father!" Elisha cried out. But he saw his master no more.

The mantle which had fallen from Elijah lay on the ground. Elisha took it up, and returned across the Jordan.

When the prophets who were at Jericho saw him coming, they said, "The spirit of Elijah rests on Elisha."

People say that Elijah never died. They say that he still returns to earth, to help people in their need. Any day he may knock upon one's door disguised as a poor stranger. We sing songs to him at the close of the Sabbath. On Passover, we open the door and invite him in.

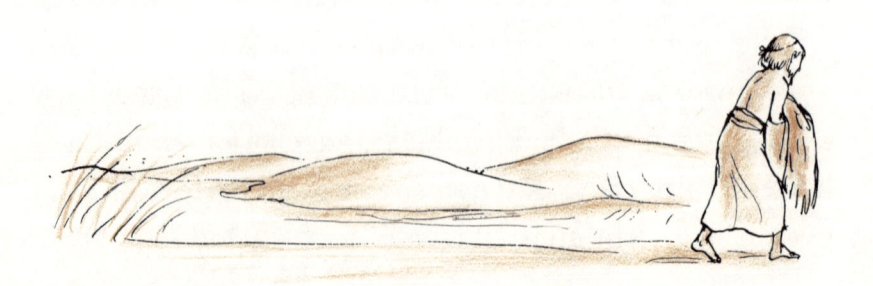

The Story of Amos

Amos the Shepherd

IN THE VILLAGE of Tekoa, south of Jerusalem, there once lived a shepherd named Amos. Amos tended his sheep in the rocky pastures in the hills. It was a wild and lonely place. Everything around him made Amos think of God. The high mountains, the winds, the sudden storms that darkened the sky—God had made them all.

At night Amos wrapped himself in his rough cloak and lay down among the sheep. Overhead the stars moved slowly across the heavens.

"God made the stars," Amos said. "He turns the darkest night into morning."

There were seasons when Amos went down into the valley to work in the groves of sycamore trees. A kind of fig, that poor folk used, grew on these sycamores. The fruit was small, but sweet and plentiful.

Often, as Amos went about his work, long lines of camels passed in the distance. They carried merchants and their goods. Sometimes the camel drivers came to the grove to re-fill their water jars. They spoke of the far lands from which they had come, of kings and wars, of splendid cities, of the rich goods their masters carried, gold and ivory and spices.

Amos had much to think about when he went back to his sheep.

"These many lands and peoples," he said, "God rules over them all. The nations do not know it, but the Lord is their God also. He is God of all the earth."

One day in the spring, after the sheep had been sheared, Amos set out for Beth El to sell his wool in the market. Beth El, you remember, was the place where Jacob once dreamed of a ladder that reached to heaven. But that was a long, long time before Amos was born. Now Beth El was a great city with busy streets and markets and temples.

Amos walked through the crowded streets, noticing everything with his keen eyes, and listening to the talk of the people. Slave traders with cruel faces spoke of wars in the north. Fine ladies stood at the stalls, buying jeweled bands, earrings, perfumes. Golden anklets tinkled on their feet. All around them were women and children who were ragged and without shoes.

Into the grand houses, servants carried whole sheep, ready for roasting. But in the market, poor men bargained for a bit of bread for their families. And Amos saw that the merchants cheated them. Anger took hold of him.

"Your scales are false," he cried to one of the merchants. "You make the measures too small and the price too high."

He turned to the poor man who had been cheated, saying, "Go to the judges and complain."

The poor man answered, "The judges do not listen to us. They take bribes from the rich."

Amos sold his wool and returned to his village. But he could not forget what he had seen. Often in the early morning as he set out with his sheep, he would stop on the hill top to look across the valley. Far in the distance, he could see the Dead Sea shining in the sun. Once the cities of Sodom and Gomorrah had stood in that very place. God had destroyed them for their wickedness.

Amos thought, "If the cities of Israel do not turn from their evil ways, they, too, will be destroyed."

Then Amos heard the voice of God speak to him. "Leave your flocks. Go to Beth El and Samaria, to all the cities of Israel, and say to the people what I will tell you to say."

Hate Evil and Love Good

Again Amos stood in a crowded market place. This time it was the market place of Samaria where Ahab had once lived. People hurried by, each one interested in his own affairs.

Suddenly Amos cried aloud, "Punishment is coming upon Damascus. Because of the cruelty of its people, God will not turn it back. Punishment is coming upon the Philistines! Punishment is coming upon Edom and Moab."

The people stopped and listened eagerly, for Damascus and Edom and Moab were Israel's old enemies.

But now Amos cried, "Punishment is coming upon *you*, O men of Israel. You oppress the poor. You keep the weak from getting justice."

The people no longer looked pleased. It was one thing for this stranger to speak against their enemies. It was another thing for him to prophesy against *them*.

Someone in the crowd shouted, "Do not listen to this trouble maker. Will God let harm come to His own people?"

Amos answered, "*All* peoples belong to God. God brought the children of Israel out of Egypt. He also brought the Philistines and Damascans from the lands where *they* were slaves. O men of Israel, do you truly wish to be God's people? Then hate evil and love good."

From Samaria Amos went up to Beth El. It was a feast day and the temple courts were crowded. Rich and poor had come to bring their offerings. Musicians played on harps and lyres.

Amos stood on the temple steps and began singing a sad, wailing chant. His mournful voice rose above the talk and the music and the bleating of lambs. People turned toward Amos, startled. Who was this stranger who dared to sing a funeral chant in the temple? For whom was he mourning? They listened to his words.

"Fallen, never to rise again
    Is the daughter of Israel."

The stranger was mourning for *them!*

Now that a crowd had gathered Amos stopped singing and spoke to the peoples: "A nation from the north is coming to destroy you. This very temple will lie in ruins."

Pointing to the altars where priests were sacrificing young bulls and lambs, Amos said, "Do not think that God will save you because you bring Him offerings. God says to you, 'I hate, I despise your feasts. I will not accept your offerings, because you hurt innocent people, and take bribes, and turn your backs on those who are in need.'"

The high priest, dressed in splendid robes, hurried up to Amos.

"You dreamer," he said, "be off to the land of Judah where you came from. If you *must* prophesy to earn your living, be a prophet there, but do not come to Beth El to prophesy. This is the king's temple and a royal house."

Amos answered, "I am no prophet who speaks for pay. I am a shepherd and a tender of sycamore trees. And the Lord took me from my sheep and said, 'Go, prophesy to my people Israel.' *You* say, 'Do not prophesy against Israel.' But *God* says, 'Israel shall surely be carried away captive, far from her own land.' "

Then Amos turned and left the temple. A few of the people followed him, troubled by his words.

One asked, "Why do you speak so harshly of the people of Israel? We are no worse than our neighbors."

Amos answered him sternly, "Is it enough for Israel to be 'no worse'? Was it for this that God brought us out of Egypt and gave us His commandments? God says, 'To you alone of all the nations of the earth I made Myself known. Therefore, *you*, more than all others, must keep My commandments.' "

Still the people questioned him, "O, prophet, tell us what we should do?"

This time Amos' voice was gentle as he answered,

"Let justice well up as water,
 And righteousness as a mighty stream.
 Then God may yet save Israel."

After this Amos spoke no more in Israel, but returned to his flocks in Judah. But God sent other prophets to bring His word to the people.

The Story of Isaiah

How Isaiah Became a Prophet

ISAIAH WAS the son of a Jewish prince. All his life he lived in the city of Jerusalem. Isaiah loved his city, set high on a mountain like a crown. To Jerusalem, long ago, King David had brought the ark of the Lord. Here Solomon had built the Holy Temple, which was still standing. Jerusalem seemed to Isaiah like a princess, the daughter of Zion. He wanted it to be pure and holy just as God was holy.

But the people of Jerusalem were *not* pure and holy. Walking through its crowded streets, Isaiah saw all the evils that Amos had seen in Beth El and Samaria. The men of Judah broke God's commandments. They hurt one another. They made their lips unclean with lying words.

"And I am no better than the others," Isaiah thought. "If I were, I would not be silent. My lips would cry out against the evil."

One day, deeply troubled by his thoughts, Isaiah went to the Holy Temple to pray. There a vision came to him. It was like a dream, except that he was awake. In his vision, angels were calling to one another,

> "Holy, holy, holy is the Lord of Hosts.
> The whole earth is full of His glory."

The Temple trembled at their voices.

"Woe is me," Isaiah cried, "for I am a man of unclean lips. And I dwell among a people of unclean lips."

Then an angel flew down with a burning coal which he had taken from the altar. He touched Isaiah's mouth with it, saying, "Lo, this has touched your lips. The evil in you is removed. Your sin is forgiven."

Then Isaiah heard the voice of God saying,

> "Whom shall I send?
> Who will go for us?"

Isaiah answered: "Here I am. Send me."

Thus Isaiah became a prophet. Wherever people gathered, in the streets, in the market place, in the Temple Courts, Isaiah brought God's word.

He said to the merchants who grew rich by cheating,

"God says to you, 'What do you mean by crushing My people?' "

He spoke to their vain and selfish wives. They walked with little mincing steps, their anklets tinkling, their heads held proudly. All they thought of was their clothes and jewels, their earrings and bracelets, their veils and embroidered sashes, their perfume boxes and signet rings.

Isaiah warned them and pleaded with them:

> "Share your food with the hungry.
> Clothe the naked.
> Bring the homeless into your homes."

He spoke against the judges who accepted bribes, against the powerful landowners who took away the poor farmers' fields. Wherever a wrong was done, Isaiah spoke out fearlessly.

In time people began to listen to Isaiah's words. A small band of faithful followers gathered about him.

Return to Your God

A son was born to Isaiah. Isaiah gave him a strange, long name—Shaar-yeshub. Now, *shaar* means *a part of something*, a *remnant*, and *yeshub* means *shall return*.

Isaiah's followers said to him, "*Shaar-yeshub*, a *Rem-*

nant-shall-return. What made you give the child this strange name?"

Isaiah said to them, "God told me to give my son this name. It is to be a reminder to us, a sign of hope. No matter how many of the people of Judah turn away from God to do evil, we must not lose hope. Shaar-yeshub! A part of them, a remnant, will turn back. Even if our enemies come and carry us away to a strange land, we must not lose hope. Shaar-yeshub! A remnant, the faithful ones, will return."

Shaar-yeshub was still very young when his father began taking the boy about with him. Whenever Isaiah spoke, crowds gathered to listen. Once, on a busy market day, Shaar-yeshub stood with his father near the gates of the city. Farmers were coming in from the country, their donkeys laden with baskets of grapes, freshly picked from the vines.

Suddenly Isaiah began calling out to the passersby:

"Come, let me sing you a song,
  A song about my friend and his vineyard."

People drew close, for every one loves a song that tells a story. Then Isaiah sang them a song about a friend who had a vineyard on a fruitful hill. He dug it, and cleared it of stones, and planted the finest vines. And he tended his vineyard and watched over it, expecting it to grow good grapes. Instead it grew wild grapes.

"Tell me, men of Judah," Isaiah said to his listeners, "could my friend have done any more for his vineyard than he did? Why, then, when he looked for good grapes, did he find bad ones?"

When no one answered, Isaiah said, "I will tell you what my friend will do with his vineyard. He will stop weeding and pruning it. It will be choked with thorns and thistles. He will take away the fence and it will be trampled upon."

The vine-growers in the crowd nodded their heads. "Your friend is right," they said. "Why should he trouble himself with worthless vines?"

Suddenly Isaiah's voice changed. Looking straight into the faces of the people, he cried, "Men of Judah, *you* are the vineyard of the Lord."

Shaar-yeshub, who was listening, understood what his father meant. God was like the friend in the story, and

Israel like the vineyard. God had cared for Israel and watched over it and protected it from its enemies, expecting His children to do what was good and right. But many of them did *not* do what was good and right. They lied and cheated and hurt one another.

"What will God do now?" Shaar-yeshub wondered. "Will he let our enemies come and carry us away?"

He felt his father's hand resting on his head. Isaiah's voice had grown quiet and gentle.

"O, my people," he pleaded, "return to your God.

> Cease to do evil,
> Learn to do good.
> Then God will again call you His beloved vine.
> He will guard you night and day."

The King Who Had No Faith

It happened at this time that the northern kingdom of Israel joined with a neighboring kingdom to make war against Judah. Messengers brought the news to King Ahaz at he sat in his palace in Jerusalem.

"The king of Israel has joined with the king of Aram. Their armies are coming up against Jerusalem!"

"The soldiers have set fire to our crops. They are carrying off our women and children. Thousands of our men have been slain."

The hearts of King Ahaz and the people trembled as the trees of the forest tremble before the wind.

"There is but one thing for us to do," the princes of Judah said. "We must send messengers to the king of Assyria and beg him to come to our help."

Assyria was a mighty kingdom in the north. Its people were fierce, and warlike, and cruel. Its army was the strongest in the world.

"Only the king of Assyria can help us," the princes said.

But Isaiah knew that Judah must turn to God for help, not to the cruel Assyrian king. Now the father of King Ahaz had been a good king, a friend of the prophets. Isaiah hoped that the son, too, would listen to God's words. So he took his little son, Shaar-yeshub, and went to find the king.

King Ahaz and the princes were talking excitedly about the water supply. They knew that once the enemy surrounded the city walls, it would be impossible to bring in any more water or food.

Isaiah, with his little son, went up to them.

"Keep calm. Have no fear," he said to King Ahaz.

And he spoke scornfully of the two kings who had come against them, calling them two smoking firebrands (sticks of burning wood).

Shaar-yeshub had often seen a stick of wood pulled out of the fire. It made a big blaze and much smoke, but was soon burned out.

He said to himself, "My father must think the kings are not so strong as they seem."

Shaar-yeshub listened again. Now Isaiah was talking earnestly to King Ahaz and the princes.

"The kings from the north have plotted together, saying, 'Let us go up against Jerusalem, and terrify it, and put a king of our own on its throne.' But God says, 'The plot shall not succeed. The plot shall fail.' Ahaz, ask for a sign from God that you may believe me."

But Ahaz did not want to believe. He had already made up his mind to turn to the Assyrian king.

"I will not ask," he said.

"Then God himself will give you a sign," Isaiah said, and he pointed to a young woman who was standing near by. "Behold, the young woman is to bear a child. She shall call him Emanuel (God-is-with-us). Before he is old enough to know the difference between good and evil, the lands of these kings you dread shall be forsaken. If you do not have faith, Ahaz, your kingdom will not last."

But King Ahaz did *not* have faith.

He sent messengers to the king of Assyria, saying, "I will be your servant. Come and save me from the enemies who have surrounded my city."

Then the king of Assyria sent his armies against the kingdoms of Israel and Aram, and their kings had to leave Jerusalem and hurry home to defend their own cities. But in return for this help, King Ahaz was forced to give up all the gold and silver in the Temple, all the treasures of the palace.

Nor was this all that Ahaz did. Since the days of King Solomon there had been an altar to God in the court of the Temple. To please the Assyrian king, King Ahaz removed this altar. In its place, he built an altar to the cruel gods of Assyria. The image of a war horse stood beside it. All through the land altars were set up to honor the cruel gods of Assyria, and the people of Judah turned farther and farther from God's ways. These were sad days for Isaiah and his followers.

But all the while a little prince was growing up in the palace who would one day turn the people back to God.

The Good King Hezekiah

The name of the little prince was Hezekiah. He was a son of King Ahaz. Hezekiah's mother feared and hated the religion which her husband had copied from the Assyrians. Her own eyes had seen how dreadful and cruel it could be. It was through the queen that Isaiah came to know the little prince.

"Tell me about my grandfather," Hezekiah would say to him.

And Isaiah would tell the prince stories about his good grandfather, how he served God faithfully and was the prophets' friend.

Hezekiah would say, "When I am king, I will be like my grandfather. I will tear down the dreadful altars in the valley. Every child, from Dan to Beersheba, shall know God's laws."

Isaiah spoke to his followers of the little crown prince whose heart had turned to God.

"A son has been given to us," he said joyfully. "Some day he will rule over the land."

The day came at last when Hezekiah was made king over Judah. It was a day of joy and gladness for Isaiah and his followers. The first thing the young king did was to break down the altars to the false gods. Then he sent word throughout the land that all the people were to come up to Jerusalem to celebrate the Passover. Crowds of happy people streamed through the Temple gates, singing and bringing offerings. Never since the days of King Solomon had there been so joyful a *Pesach*.

Hezekiah ruled the people justly and wisely. He listened to the words of Isaiah and tried to follow in God's ways.

God Saves Jerusalem

The words of the prophets came true. Assyria conquered the northern kingdom of Israel, and carried the people away captive. But it did not stop with Israel. Country after country fell before its dread armies. Now, Assyrian commanders stood before the gates of Jerusalem calling for King Hezekiah to surrender. Behind them stretched an endless army, footmen and horsemen, fighters with shields and spears, with bows and arrows.

King Hezekiah sent out three of his officers to talk with the enemy.

They said to the Assyrians, "Please speak to us in your

own language, for we understand it. Do not speak in Hebrew. The soldiers on the wall may hear you."

The Assyrian commander answered insolently, "Let your soldiers hear us. It is *they* who will soon be dying of hunger and thirst."

Raising his voice louder, he shouted in Hebrew, "Hear the word of the great king, the king of Assyria. Why should you die, men of Judah? Give your city up, and your lives will be spared. Do not listen to King Hezekiah when he says, 'The Lord will save you.' Has the god of any nation saved his people from the king of Assyria? Did the Lord save your brothers in the kingdom of Israel?"

The people remained silent, answering not a word.

The words of the enemy were reported to King Hezekiah, and he mourned and put on sackcloth, and hurried to the Temple. From the Temple he sent a message to Isaiah, "This is a day of sorrow and disgrace. The king of Assyria has sent his officers to insult the living God. Pray for the people of Judah that are left."

Isaiah's answer came back quickly.

"Have no fear and do not surrender. Say to the king of Assyria,

> 'Jerusalem despises you
> And laughs you to scorn.
> Whom have you insulted,
> Against whom have you lifted your voice?
> Against God, the Holy One of Israel?
> Therefore the Lord God says:

"The king of Assyria shall not enter the city. He shall not shoot an arrow into it. By the way he came, shall he return. I, the Lord, will defend Jerusalem."

That night a strange sickness broke out in the camp of the Assyrians. When morning came, thousands of Assyrian soldiers lay dead. The king of Assyria fled to his own land. There in his temple as he was praying to his false gods, two of his own sons killed him.

Swords into Plows

King Hezekiah ruled over Judah for many years. He was a good and just king. But his son was not like him. As soon as Hezekiah's son became king, he forbade the prophets to teach. Again altars were set up to honor the false gods.

Isaiah's followers came to him in their discouragement.

"One king is good," they said, "but the next king does evil, and none is perfect. Men go on hurting one another, and nations are at war."

Isaiah was now an old man. He had lived long enough to see four kings rule over Judah. But his faith was as firm as on the day God called him in the Temple.

He said to his followers what he had said to them many times before,

> "It will not always be so.
> A day will come when
> Nations will beat their swords into plows,
> And their spears into pruning hooks.
> Nation shall not lift up sword against nation,
> Neither shall they learn war anymore."

"When will that day be?" the people asked.

Isaiah answered, "It will be long, long in coming. But it will surely come. In that day men will no more hurt one another, for the earth shall be full of the knowledge of the Lord as the waters cover the sea."

The Story of Jeremiah

Jeremiah Becomes a Prophet

MANY YEARS had passed since Isaiah brought God's word to the people of Judah.

In the village of Anatoth, not far from Jerusalem, a boy named Jeremiah sat in the doorway of his home. He was the little son of a *Kohen*. From the doorstep Jeremiah could see his neighbors, busily at work. The children gathered sticks and the father built a fire. Now the mother was baking small moonshaped cakes. The smell of the baking cakes came to Jeremiah in the breeze. He knew why the cakes were moon-shaped. It was because they were to be brought as offerings to the moon goddess, whose altar was hidden in the grove of trees outside the town.

Jeremiah's forehead wrinkled in a puzzled frown.

These neighbors were children of Israel just as he was. Why, then, did they bring offerings to the moon goddess? Did they not know God's commandment: *I am the Lord thy God. Thou shalt have no other gods before Me.*

As Jeremiah grew older other things troubled him. Once his father stopped to speak to a Hebrew slave who passed their house. The slave's back was bent beneath a heavy load.

Jeremiah's father sighed when the man had gone.

"That was an old neighbor of ours," he said. "Once he borrowed money to buy seed and food. When he could not pay his debt, he was sold as a slave. Seven years he has served his master."

"But father," Jeremiah said, "if he has served for seven years, his master will set him free. That is the law."

Again his father sighed.

"The rich men do not keep the law," he said.

Jeremiah could not forget this Hebrew slave, who would never be free because his master did not keep God's law.

One day he was thinking about the slave and about other things that troubled him. Suddenly he heard the voice of God calling him.

"Jeremiah, I have chosen you to be a prophet."

"O Lord God," Jeremiah answered, "I cannot speak. I am too young."

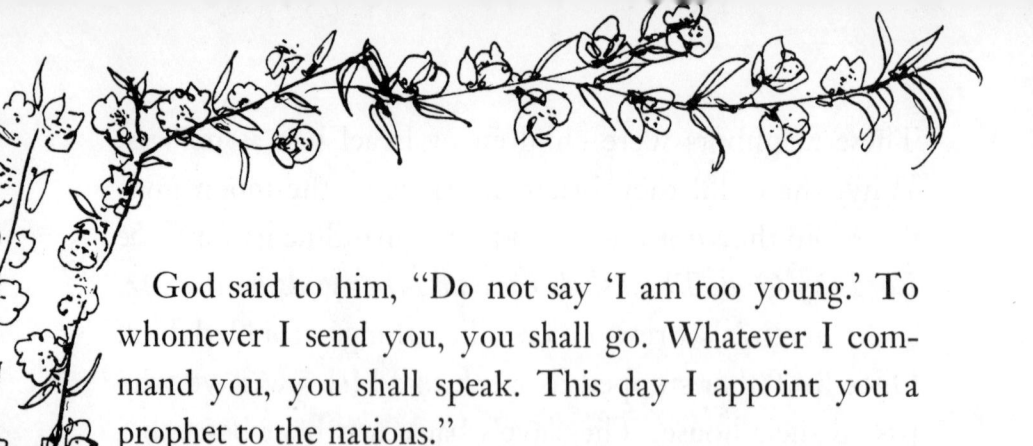

God said to him, "Do not say 'I am too young.' To whomever I send you, you shall go. Whatever I command you, you shall speak. This day I appoint you a prophet to the nations."

Springtime came. One day the twigs on the trees looked like brown sticks. The next day the almond twigs were covered with buds.

Again Jeremiah heard the voice of God.

"What do you see, Jeremiah?" God asked him.

"I see the twig of an almond tree," he answered. "It is ready to blossom."

God said to him, "You have seen well. I, too, am ready to fulfill my promise."

A second time Jeremiah heard God ask, "What do you see, Jeremiah?"

This time Jeremiah answered, "I see a pot boiling over. It is tipped from the north."

God said, "Out of the north trouble is boiling over. Go up to Jerusalem and say to the people what I will tell you to say. Do not keep back one word."

It was hard for the shy and gentle Jeremiah to leave

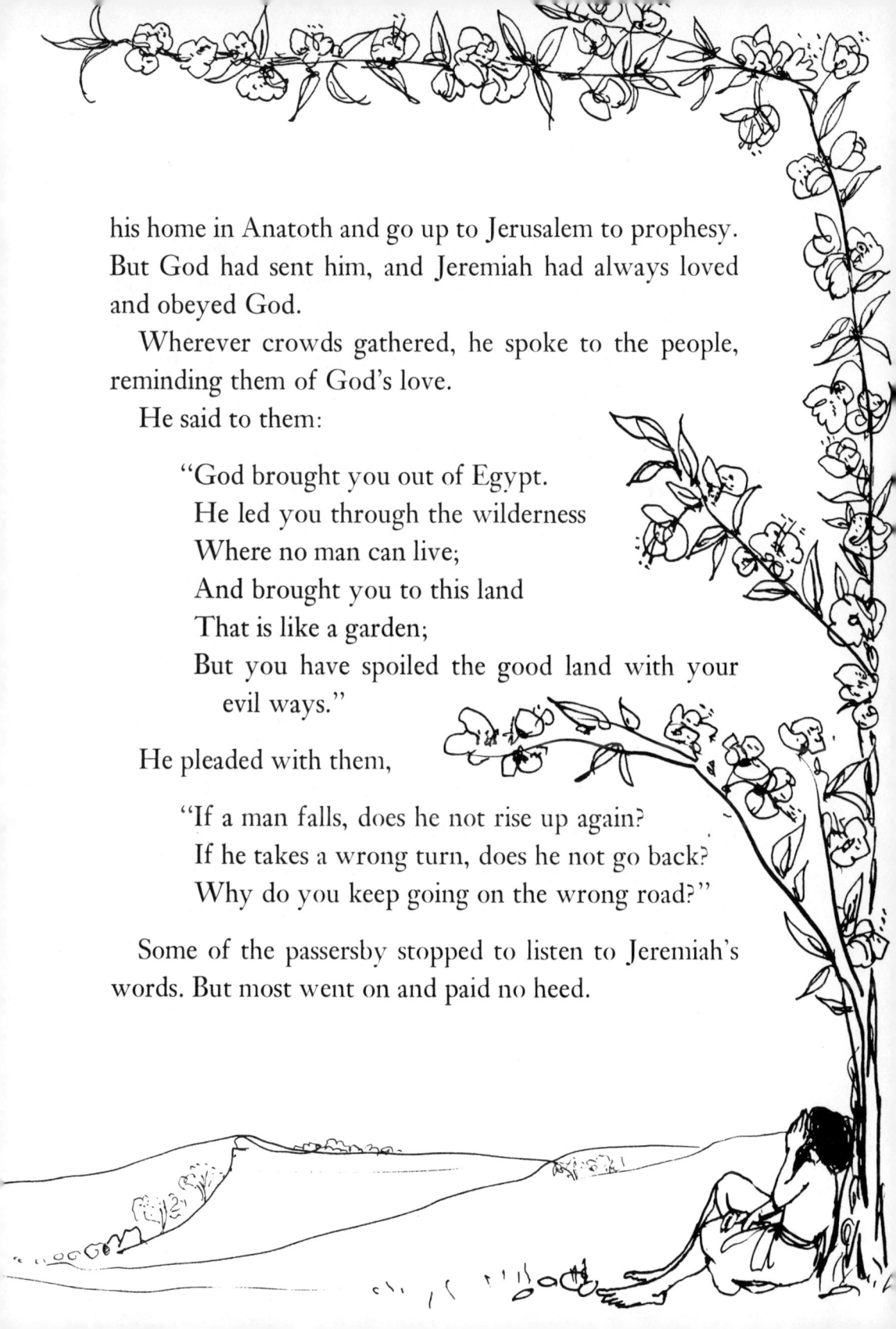

his home in Anatoth and go up to Jerusalem to prophesy. But God had sent him, and Jeremiah had always loved and obeyed God.

Wherever crowds gathered, he spoke to the people, reminding them of God's love.

He said to them:

> "God brought you out of Egypt.
> He led you through the wilderness
> Where no man can live;
> And brought you to this land
> That is like a garden;
> But you have spoiled the good land with your evil ways."

He pleaded with them,

> "If a man falls, does he not rise up again?
> If he takes a wrong turn, does he not go back?
> Why do you keep going on the wrong road?"

Some of the passersby stopped to listen to Jeremiah's words. But most went on and paid no heed.

The Burning of the Scroll

A day came when Jeremiah could no longer speak gently to the people. A new kingdom had arisen in the north, the kingdom of Babylonia. It conquered Israel's old enemy, Assyria, but it also conquered every other country in its way. Nearer and nearer it drew to Judah.

Jeremiah's heart ached as he warned the people;

> A destroyer of nations is coming.
> His chariots are like a whirlwind.
> His horses are swifter than eagles.
>
> Your own doings have brought this upon you.
> O, Jerusalem, turn from your wickedness
> That you may be saved.

There were false prophets who laughed at Jeremiah's warnings. "Jerusalem will never be destroyed," they said. "Is not the Lord's Temple in Jerusalem? God will not let harm come to his own Temple."

The people repeated these words, saying, "The Temple of the Lord will save us. There is nothing to fear." And they went on lying and cheating and hurting one another.

Then Jeremiah stood in the gates of the Temple and cried aloud, "Do not trust in the lying words, 'The Temple of the Lord will save you.' Will you steal and murder and lie and bring sacrifices to Baal, and then come before God in this House and think that you are safe? Do you think God's Temple is a den of robbers? God says to you, 'If you change your ways, if you stop hurting the stranger and the fatherless and the widow, and do justice to one another, then I will let you stay in this land forever. If not, I will cast you out. This very Temple will be destroyed.'"

An angry shout went up from the crowd. The priests and the people took hold of Jeremiah.

"You shall die," they shouted. "How dare you say that the Temple will be destroyed."

The princes in the palace heard the commotion and hurried to the Temple.

"The man must have a trial," they said. And they saved Jeremiah from the hands of the mob.

Then they sat down at one of the gates to judge him.

The priests spoke first.

"This man deserves to die," they said. "He says our Temple will be destroyed. You heard him with your own ears."

Jeremiah turned to the judges and the people.

"It is the Lord who sent me to prophesy against the Temple and the city. I am in your power. Do with me as you think right and good. But if you kill me, you will be spilling innocent blood."

Then the judges said, "This man does not deserve to die. He has spoken to us in the name of the Lord our God."

So Jeremiah's life was spared. But he was forbidden to speak again in the Temple.

What could Jeremiah do now? He had been forbidden to return to the Temple. Yet he knew that he must bring God's message to the people. If they heard it, they might turn from their evil ways and be saved. He sent for his faithful friend Baruch.

"Baruch," he said, "take ink and a scroll and write down what I tell you."

Then he dictated to Baruch all the words that God had spoken to him from the day he had become a prophet.

When the words had been carefully written down, Jeremiah said to Baruch, "Tomorrow is a fast day. Many people will be coming up to Jerusalem from every town of Judah. Go to the Temple and read aloud what is written in the scroll."

Baruch did as Jeremiah had said. Standing in a room whose window looked down into the Temple court, he read aloud from the scrolls. A great dread fell upon the people as they heard God's warnings. Baruch was taken to the palace and asked to read the scroll again, this time before the princes. When he had finished, the princes looked at one another in alarm.

"Tell us how you came to write these words," they said.

"Jeremiah dictated them to me," Baruch answered.

"Go into hiding, you and Jeremiah," said the princes. "Let no one know where you are."

Then they brought the scroll to the king. It was winter and the king was sitting before a fire. The princes watched him anxiously as the scroll was read. They saw no fear in his eyes, no sign of sorrow, only scorn and anger. Each time a few columns had been read, the king slashed them off with his knife and flung them into the fire until the whole scroll had been burned. Then he commanded his servants.

"Arrest Baruch the scribe, and Jeremiah the prophet."

But Baruch and Jeremiah could not be found.

Now God said to Jeremiah, "Take another scroll and write on it all the words that were on the first scroll. As for the king, send him this message: 'You have burned the scroll, but what was written in the scroll shall surely come to pass.'"

Jerusalem Is Destroyed

What was written in the scroll *did* come to pass. A day came when a mighty Babylonian army stood outside the gates of Jerusalem. It threw up mounds of earth to ring the city round. It battered at the walls with huge rock-throwing machines.

Now at last, the people remembered Jeremiah's warnings.

They said to one another, "Jeremiah told us to be just to one another. He told us that we must let our slaves go free. But we would not listen. It is because we broke God's laws that this trouble has come to us."

By this time there was a new king in Jerusalem. The king called a great assembly and the people prayed to God and promised to give up their evil ways. Every man who owned a Hebrew slave let his slave go free.

Suddenly the enemy broke camp and marched away.

"We are saved," the people cried joyfully. "The danger is past."

At once they forgot their prayers and their promises. "There was really no need to give up our slaves," they said, and each man hurried after the slaves that he had freed and forced them back. Then Jeremiah knew that there was no more hope for Judah.

Rising before the leaders of the city he cried aloud: "Did not God bring our fathers out of Egypt, the land of slavery? Did he not command us, 'Proclaim liberty throughout the land.' But you have taken back the slaves that you set free. Therefore, God says, 'The Babylonians shall return, and you yourselves shall be carried off in chains.'"

After he had spoken, Jeremiah turned his back on the angry princes and set out for Anatoth. At the gate of the city the sentry stopped him.

"Halt," he cried. "You are deserting to the enemy."

"It is false," Jeremiah said.

But the princes arrested him and had him imprisoned in the palace.

The Babylonians soon were back. Again the city was surrounded. Month after month Jerusalem was shut in by the enemy. The hot, dry days of summer came. No rain fell to fill the cisterns. No food or water could be brought in. Showers of arrows struck down the fighters on the wall. But there were more who died inside the city from hunger and thirst and sickness.

In the palace prison, people kept coming to Jeremiah.

"Jeremiah," they pleaded, "tell us what the end will be."

Jeremiah's heart was torn with pity for his people. He loved them in spite of all their faults. He longed to comfort them, to answer, "All will be well. Jerusalem will be saved." But he knew this was not so, and he had to speak the truth.

The princes hurried to the king.

"Jeremiah is discouraging the people," they said. "He is on the side of the enemy. Let him he put to death."

The king knew that Jeremiah was loyal, but he feared the princes.

He answered them, "Do with Jeremiah as you will."

So Jeremiah was seized and lowered into an empty cistern. There at the bottom of the pit, without food, without water, sunk deep in mud, he waited for death. Suddenly, he heard a voice calling to him. He looked up and saw one of the king's servants, a tall, black Ethiopian, kneeling near the cistern. The servant had gone to the king, pleading for the prophet's life.

"Here are some rags and a rope," he called to Jeremiah. "Put the rope below your armpits with the rags between. We have come to save you."

Thus Jeremiah was saved from the pit and brought secretly before the king.

"Have you any message for me from the Lord?" the king asked anxiously. "You must not hide anything from me."

Jeremiah answered, "If I give you advice, will you listen? If I tell you the truth, will you not put me to death?"

The king said, "I swear that I will neither put you to death not turn you over to the princes."

Then Jeremiah said, "There is but one way by which Jerusalem can be saved. If you surrender to the king of Babylonia, the city will be left standing. If not, the city will be burned to the ground."

But the king was too much afraid of the princes to listen to Jeremiah's words.

God Comforts Jeremiah

In the month of Tammuz, a break was made in the walls of Jerusalem and the enemy rushed in. The Babylonian soldiers fought their way street by street. Deeper and deeper into the city they went, killing and plundering and burning. On the ninth day of the month of Ab, the Holy Temple, which had stood in Jerusalem since the days of King Solomon, went up in flames.

The king with his wife and sons fled out of the city by a secret passage, down to the Jordan valley. But the Babylonian soldiers pursued him and caught him near Jericho. Blinded and bound in chains, he was taken to Babylonia. With him went thousands and thousands of men and women and little children, driven along the road by cruel Babylonian soldiers.

Jeremiah had been left behind. He sat beside the ruins of Jerusalem, bowed with sorrow. Tears streamed down his cheeks. He was an old man now. All his life he had longed to live quietly, to be at peace with his people. Yet, all his life he had had to warn and threaten them. No prophet had been so lonely, so full of sorrow. But Jeremiah was not weeping for himself. He was mourning for Jerusalem and for his people who had been taken captive.

"How lonely is the city,
　　Once so full of people.
　She that was a princess among the nations
　　Has become a captive."

Mourning, Jeremiah fell asleep, and a dream came to him. In his dream, he heard a voice of bitter weeping.

"It is the voice of Rachel," he said in wonder. "Mother Rachel is weeping for her children. She refuses to be comforted."

Then Jeremiah heard the voice of God saying:

> "Do not weep.
>   Your children shall come back from the land
>   of the enemy.
>   There is hope for your future.
>   Your children shall return to their own land."

At this Jeremiah awoke.

"How sweet was my sleep," he said. Now he understood what God would bring to pass. In that far land to which his people had been taken, they would turn to God as they had not turned to Him in their own land. With all their hearts they would seek Him. And a day would come when God would bring them back. Again farmers would plant and reap, and shepherds tend their flocks in the hill country and in the southlands. Again sounds of singing and gladness would be heard in the streets of Jerusalem, and in all the cities of Judah and of Israel.

Leaders of the Exile and the Return

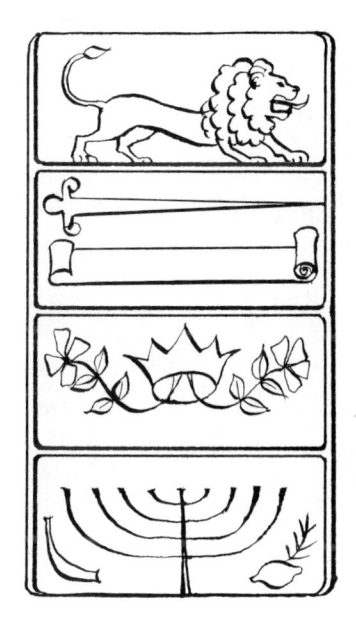

DANIEL

EZRA AND NEHEMIAH

ESTHER

JUDAH MACCABEE

The Story of Daniel

Daniel Is Brought to the Palace

NEBUCHADNEZZAR, king of Babylonia, conqueror of Judah, sat in his royal palace in the city of Babylon. He was giving orders to the chief officer of his household.

"It is my plan," said the king, "to have a number of the Judean captives educated in our royal school. Go and choose them for me. See to it that they are lads who belong to the royal family or to the nobles, all healthy, handsome, well mannered, quick to learn. After they have spent three years in the palace, you are to bring them before me."

The officer set out at once for the Judean settlement. All youths were brought before him. He talked to one, to another. He went back to the first. He talked to a third and a fourth. He turned again to the first.

"What is your name?" he asked.

"Daniel," said the lad.

"Where do you come from?"

"From Judah."

"What is your father's name?"

Daniel named one of the princes of Judah.

"H'm," said the Babylonian officer checking the words off on his fingers. "The king said the lads were to be well born, well mannered, educated, handsome, healthy, bright—. This lad has everything."

So Daniel was the first to be chosen. Three other youths from Judah, all friends of Daniel, were among the rest.

The lads looked about them in wonder as they followed the king's officer. He led them down a long avenue between gleaming walls of tile. The walls were decorated with marching lions; the gateway at the end of the avenue with winged bulls. Beyond the gate was the palace of the king. Never had the youths seen so splendid a palace. Its golden walls dazzled their eyes. Its doorways glittered in the sun. But it was not the palace that held Daniel's eyes. It was the temple that rose beyond it. Up and up and up towered the temple, platform above platform. Its zig zag stairways seemed climbing to the sky. This was the temple of the Babylonian god, Bel.

Daniel turned to his friends.

"I will learn the language of these Babylonians and study in their books," he said to them. "I will serve their king faithfully. He took us from our homes in Judah, but now he is kind to us. But there is one thing that I will *not* do. I will not turn away from the religion of our fathers."

"Nor will we," said the three friends.

That very day they were put to the test. It was soon after the youths had been led to their rooms near the palace. Servants entered bearing trays of steaming meats, roasts, stuffed ducks and geese. Other servants carried pastries and sweets and jars of wine. Cups were filled, plates piled with food. The hungry youths ate with relish —all but Daniel and his friends. These four left their plates untouched.

The officer of the king hurried toward them. He had taken a special liking to Daniel.

"Eat, my son," he said. "This is meat and wine from the king's own table."

Daniel answered, "My lord, the meat is not prepared according to our laws. I beg you to excuse me from eating."

But the officer shook his head.

"The king has put you in my care," he said. "If he finds that you look worse than the other lads of your age, he will hold me responsible."

Daniel answered, "I beg you, test us for ten days. Give us only vegetables to eat and water to drink. Then compare our looks with that of the others who eat the king's meat. Your own eyes will tell you what to do."

The officer agreed to the test. At the end of the ten days he saw that Daniel and his friends looked better than all the others. So he kept on bringing them only vegetables to eat.

For three years the youths remained in the palace school. They learned to read and write the language of Babylonia. They studied the stars and the meaning of dreams. They learned the secrets of the wise men written on old clay tablets.

When the three years had passed, the keeper of the palace brought them before the king. Nebuchadnezzar questioned them one by one. He found none to compare with Daniel and his three friends in wisdom and knowledge. So these four were asked to stay on in the palace with the wise men of the king.

The Stone That Became a Mountain

One morning Nebuchadnezzar arose from his sleep, deeply troubled.

He said to his wisemen, "I have dreamed a dream that will not let me rest."

The wisemen answered, "O king, live forever. Tell us your dream and we will tell you its meaning."

But the king answered, "I do not remember the dream. *You* must tell me what it was. After that, you shall explain its meaning."

"The king asks an impossible thing," the wisemen protested. "There is not a man on earth, not a priest nor magician, who can tell a man his dream. No king, however mighty, has ever asked such a thing."

At this the king became so angry that he sent for the captain of his guard and ordered him to put to death all the wisemen in the kingdom.

The captain set out and the first wiseman he met was Daniel.

"I must put you to death," he said. "It is the king's order."

Daniel said, "Why must you hurry? First tell me why the king has given this harsh command."

The captain told him what had happened.

Then Daniel said, "Before you destroy the wisemen of Babylon take me to the king. It may be that I will be able to tell the king's dream."

The captain agreed. That night Daniel prayed to God to help him. In the morning he was brought before the king.

The king said to him, "Are you able to tell me what my dream was?"

Daniel answered, "No man on earth could do this by himself. But there is a God in heaven who knows all things. Last night he made known to me your dream and its meaning. O king, this is the dream you dreamt. You lay on your bed wondering what was to happen in the days to come. And behold, an image stood before you—

of vast size and amazing brightness. Its head was made of gold, its breast and arms of silver, its belly of bronze, its legs of iron, its feet partly of iron and partly of clay. As you looked on, a stone was cut from the mountain—cut without hands. The stone struck the image on its feet of clay. The clay, iron, bronze, silver and gold were shattered into bits, and the wind carried them away. But the stone became a mountain and filled the earth."

Then the king cried out. "This was the very dream. Now tell me its meaning."

"O king," Daniel said, "*You* are the head of gold. The God of Heaven has given you the kingdom and the power. After you, a kingdom shall arise that is not so great as yours. Then a third kingdom shall arise, and a fourth and a fifth, each weaker than the other. In the end God will set up a kingdom that will never be destroyed, a righteous kingdom that will last forever. This righteous kingdom is the stone that became a mountain and filled the earth."

Then the king cried out, "Truly your God is the God of gods, the revealer of secrets."

And he made Daniel the first of all the wisemen of Babylon.

Nebuchadnezzar Learns a Lesson

Mightier and mightier did Nebuchadnezzar grow, and the mightier he grew the prouder he became. Again a strange dream came to him. This time he remembered the dream and told it to Daniel.

"I was lying on my bed," he said, "when I looked up and beheld a tree in the midst of the earth. It grew strong and tall until it reached the heavens. Its leaves were fair and its fruit was plentiful; giving food to all. The beasts of the field rested beneath its shade. The birds of the air nested in its branches. But even as I looked, a voice from heaven called:

> Cut down the tree and lop off its branches,
> Shake off its leaves and scatter its fruit;
> Let the beasts leave its shade
> And the birds its branches.
> Yet the stump of its roots
> Shall remain in the earth,
> 'Til seven years have passed.

"This was my dream," said the king. "Now tell me its meaning."

But Daniel stood silent and troubled.

"Do not be afraid to speak, whatever the dream may mean," the king said. "I must know the truth."

Then Daniel answered, "My king, the tree which you saw, that grew strong and spread out over the earth and gave shelter and food to man and beast—that tree is yourself. But the most high God has sent a decree against you. You shall be driven from men, and dwell with the beasts of the field, and made to eat grass as the oxen, and be wet with the dew of heaven 'til seven years have passed.

"Yet the decree is not wholly evil. There is the stump that remained in the earth. Its meaning is this: Your kingdom will remain and will be returned to you as soon as you learn that there is a God in heaven—a God who rules over the kingdom of men and gives it to whomever He will."

Then Daniel pleaded with the king. "Give charity to the poor. Show mercy and kindness to men. Then the decree may yet be set aside."

But the king would not listen to Daniel.

Twelve months passed by. One day the king was walking on the roof of his palace. The great city of Babylon spread out below him, its busy streets and markets, its canals and boats and bridges, its palaces that shone like suns, its towering temples, the seven strong walls that ringed it round, its hundred gates. Pride filled the king's heart and he said to himself, "Is not this the great city of Babylon which I have built by my own mighty power?"

The words were still in his mouth when a voice called from heaven, "O King Nebuchadnezzar, sentence has been passed upon you. Your kingdom has been taken away."

A madness fell upon the king. He was driven from among men, and ate grass like an ox, and was wet by the dew of heaven. His hair grew long as an eagle's feathers, and his nails like the claws of a bird.

So seven years passed by. Then suddenly the king's madness left him. He was brought back into the city, and his kingdom returned to him.

Thus the mighty king of Babylonia learned that the words of Daniel were true. There was a great God who ruled over the kingdom of men and it was He who had given him his power.

From that time on he no longer walked in pride, but tried to rule his people with justice and with mercy.

The Writing on the Wall

The gold and silver vessels from the holy Temple in Jerusalem lay in the king's treasure house in Babylon. Nebuchadnezzar had carried them away to Babylonia. But he would not use them, for he feared the Lord God.

In time Nebuchadnezzar died and a new king, Belshazzar, came to the throne. Belshazzar had not learned, like Nebuchadnezzar, that it was God who gave him his power. He was proud and boastful and insolent.

One night he made a great feast for a thousand of his lords. When he was drunk with wine, he ordered his servants to bring out the holy vessels from Jerusalem, and he and his princes drank out of them. While they drank the wine, they praised their gods of gold and silver and wood and stone.

Suddenly a hand appeared and began writing on the wall. The king saw it and turned pale. The cup fell from his hands, and his knees knocked against one another.

"Call the wisemen and the magicians," he cried.

When the wisemen came, the king said to them, "Whoever reads this writing and explains its meaning shall be clothed in royal robes, given a chain of gold to wear around his neck, and be the third ruler in my kingdom."

But none of the wisemen could read the writing. The king's fear grew greater, and the lords were troubled and perplexed. Then the queen mother came into the banquet hall."

"O king, live forever," she said, "do not be distressed. There is in your kingdom a man named Daniel who is filled with the spirit of God. Let Daniel be sent for."

So Daniel was called in.

King Belshazzar said to him, "I have heard that you are skilled above all others in revealing secrets. Read the writing on the wall and tell me its meaning, and you shall be clothed in royal robes, wear a chain of gold around your neck, and be the third ruler in the kingdom."

Daniel answered the king, "Keep your gifts and give your rewards to another. Yet I will read the writing and tell you its meaning. The writing comes from the Lord God. You have mocked the Lord by using the vessels of the holy Temple in your drunkenness. Hear, then, what the Lord says:

"'*Mene*'—God has numbered your kingdom and brought it to an end.

"'*Tekel*'—You have been weighed in the scales and found wanting.

"'*Ufarsin*'—Your kingdom has been divided and given to the Medes and the Persians."

That night King Belshazzar was killed in the palace. The next morning a Persian army entered the gates of Babylon. Babylonia, the conqueror of Judah, was itself conquered.

In the Lion's Den

A Persian king was now the ruler of Babylonia. He appointed one hundred and twenty princes to govern the kingdom. Over the princes he placed three presidents. One of them was Daniel.

The princes and the presidents were jealous of Daniel because of his great wisdom. They feared that the king might set him over the entire kingdom. So they watched him closely, hoping to find some fault in him that they might report to the king. But Daniel was faithful and loyal in all things.

Then the princes said, "We shall never find any cause for complaint in Daniel, unless it has something to do with the laws of his God."

Now, there was an upper room in Daniel's house which had a window looking toward Jerusalem. Three times each day Daniel knelt before this window to pray to God. This the princes knew.

So they went to the king and said to him, "O king, live forever! We, your princes and presidents, want all men to prove their loyalty to you. Therefore we have agreed on this law which we ask you to sign."

Then they took out a scroll and read from it:

"It is forbidden to offer a prayer to anyone, god or

man, for thirty days—except to the king. He who breaks this law, shall be thrown into the den of lions."

They handed the king the paper on which the law had been written, and the king signed and sealed it with his seal.

Word of the decree came to Daniel. He knew the danger he was in. Nevertheless he went on praying to God as he had always done. This was what the princes had hoped he would do.

They hurried to the king and said to him, "O king, this Daniel who was brought here as a captive from Judah, has no respect for you or your decrees. Three times a day he offers prayers to his God though it is strictly forbidden in your law. Let him be thrown to the lions."

Then the king realized that the princes had been plotting against Daniel, and he was deeply grieved. All day long he tried to find some way to save Daniel.

At sunset the princes returned saying, "O king, why are you waiting? You signed the decree, and it is a law of the Medes and the Persians that a decree signed by the king cannot be changed. Not even the king can change it."

Sadly the king gave orders that Daniel was to be brought to the lion's den. He himself went to the entrance of the den. From within came the roar of the hungry lions.

"May the Lord whom you serve so faithfully, save you," the king cried, as Daniel was thrust into the den. A rock was placed over the opening. Then it was sealed with the seal of the king and the seals of the princes.

That night the king could not sleep. As soon as it grew light he hurried to the lions' den.

"O Daniel," he cried, "has the God whom you serve so faithfully been able to save you from the lions?"

His voice was full of sorrow for he expected no answer. But out of the den came the voice of Daniel. "O king, live forever, God sent his angels to shut the mouths of the lions. They have not hurt me, for I am innocent."

Joyfully the king sent for the princes. The seals were broken and Daniel was brought forth. Not the slightest hurt was found on him.

The king gave orders that the wicked plotters be thrown to the lions. This time the mouths of the lions were *not* shut.

Daniel served the Persian king for the rest of his days, respected and honored by all.

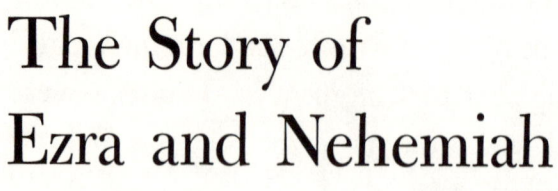

The Story of Ezra and Nehemiah

Ezra, Son of a Scribe

LITTLE EZRA, the son of a scribe in Babylonia, chose a reed pen from a pile on the table. He sharpened the tip against his thumbnail as his father had taught him. Then he dipped it into a pot of shining black ink, and began writing his name—not just Ezra, but Ezra son of Seriah, son of Azariah, son of Hilkiah—. On and on and on he went, all the way back to Aaron the high priest. Ezra was proud of all these grandfathers and great grandfathers and great-great grandfathers of his. He knew the story of every one of them.

One was the high priest in Jerusalem at the time the Babylonians destroyed the holy Temple. He stood between the enemy and the Holy of Holies. The Temple was on fire. Flames licked his robes. But he would not flee, lest the soldiers of Nebuchadnezzar enter the Holy Place.

Ezra's grandfather, now a very old man, was a young boy at the time. From him Ezra learned about the dreadful journey across the desert, and the sad days when the captives first arrived in Babylonia. With his own eyes, his grandfather had seen a letter sent to the captives by the Prophet Jeremiah. There was a verse from this letter in Ezra's copybook:

> Thus says the Lord: When seventy years have passed, I will bring you back to your own land.

The words of the prophet had come true. Long before Ezra was born, a mighty kingdom, the Kingdom of Persia, conquered Babylonia. A day came when a proclamation was read in all the Jewish settlements.

"Thus says King Cyrus, the Persian, to the Jews of Babylonia:

'Whoever there is among you who wishes to go up to Jerusalem, which is in Judah, to build the Temple of the Lord, let him go. May his God be with him. And let those who remain help with silver and gold, and supplies, and beasts of burden, and offerings for the Temple. I myself will send back the holy vessels which King Nebuchadnezzar carried away to Babylonia.'"

The people danced and sang and wept for joy. God had answered their prayers. The Jews would return to Zion. The holy Temple in Jerusalem would be rebuilt.

Forty thousand men, women and children set out on the long journey to Judea. The Jews who remained in Babylonia helped them with food and supplies, donkeys and pack mules, with rich offerings for the Temple.

Ezra's father often told him of the day the great company set forth. The people were mounted on donkeys and camels. Soldiers rode ahead to protect them. Priests carried the holy vessels of the Temple, which King Cyrus had returned. To the last moment Jews from distant parts of Babylonia came hurrying, to bring gifts of gold and silver for the rebuilding of the Temple.

Suddenly a trumpet sounded. A shout went up from all the thousands of throats, "Come, O House of Jacob, let us go up to Zion in the light of the Lord."

The great company set forth.

What happened after this, Ezra's father learned from letters and from the soldiers who returned. The journey across the desert was long and hard; the arrival in Judea even harder. Jerusalem was a heap of ruins. Rubble had to be carted away, houses built, crops planted for food. Hostile neighbors interfered with the work. The building of the Temple had to be postponed again and again. In this way many years passed.

Then one day a letter came, bringing joyful news. *The Temple was re-built at last.* This letter Ezra himself had seen. Again, as in the first Temple, a high priest in his crown and breast plate stood before God's altar. Again joyous crowds filled the holy courts. Again the Levites sang, "For His loving kindness is everlasting."

Whenever Ezra thought of it, his eyes grew bright. His heart filled wth love for God who had watched over His people, Israel, and brought them back to their land.

God's Torah

In Babylonia there was no Temple where the Jews could bring their offerings. Instead they gathered on Sabbaths and holidays to read out of the Torah scrolls and to pray. It was in this way that our synagogues began.

The Torah scroll in Ezra's synagogue was a very, very old one. It had been used in Jerusalem in the days of the first Temple. Ezra's great-grandfather, the son of the high priest, carried it with him when he was brought to Babylonia as a captive. Often, as Ezra sat in the synagogue listening to the Torah reading, he thought of the day when his great-grandfather saved the precious scroll. He could see the Temple going up in flames. He could see the long line of captives, barefoot, driven on by cruel soldiers. He could see his great-grandfather carrying the precious Torah scroll in his arms.

Ezra thought, "If the people of Judah had obeyed the commandments of the Torah, if they had listened to Jeremiah, the Temple would never have been destroyed. Nothing, *nothing* is so important as the Torah. I will learn every word of it. I will keep its laws strictly."

Ezra *did* learn and obey every law of the Torah.

He grew up to be a great scholar, a teacher, and a scribe. He found ways to bring the Torah to more and more of the people.

On Thursdays and Fridays Jewish farmers would come into town to sell their produce in the market. Ezra talked with them and saw that they knew little about the Torah. This was because there were no teachers in the small villages where they lived.

Ezra said to the townspeople, "It is not enough for us to read the Torah on Sabbaths. We must also read it on market days. Then the farmers can join us in study and prayer."

Since that time the Torah has been read on Mondays and Thursdays as well as on Sabbaths.

Books were hard to get and teachers few. Often a teacher would be glad to have a single scroll. He would unroll it on the table, while his pupils crowded around on all sides. Some of the children had to read the words side-wise, some down-side up. Some could not get near enough to read at all. Many teachers had not even *one* copy of the Torah, and there were places where there was not even a teacher.

Ezra said, "How can people keep the Torah if they do not know it?"

He gathered young men around him and taught them the Torah. These young men became teachers and scribes. They made copies of the scrolls and carried them to every settlement in the land.

Ezra Goes Up to Jerusalem

Ezra was now known throughout the land of Babylonia. Even the Persian king respected him for his wisdom. Ezra could have remained in Babylonia for the rest of his days, in comfort and honor. But the longing for Jerusalem was always in his heart. A day came when he knew that he must go up to the land of his fathers. His journey was made possible by a letter from the Persian king. The letter read:

> To Ezra, the priest, learned in the law of the God of the Heavens, greetings! Permission is given to you and to any who wish to accompany you to go up to Jerusalem. My treasurers in the lands through which you pass are to supply you with whatever you need, silver up to one hundred measures, also wheat, wine, oil and salt.

Many families decided to go up with Ezra. They camped for three days preparing for the journey. Gifts poured in from all parts of the land, offerings of gold and silver to be carried to the Temple.

"Why did you not ask the king for an armed guard?" the people said to Ezra. "We may be attacked by robber bands."

Ezra answered, "I was ashamed to ask the king for a guard. Have we not always said, 'Our God protects all who seek Him?'"

Then the people fasted, and prayed to God for a safe journey for themselves and their little ones. After five months of travel they arrived safely in Jerusalem. Joyfully they went up to the Temple to bring their offerings.

Shocking News

Three days after Ezra's arrival in Jerusalem a committee came to him. They brought shocking news. The people of Judah were again breaking God's commandments. Many of the men had taken the daughters of their neighbors for wives, women who prayed to idols; and the children followed in their mother's ways.

All day Ezra sat on the ground mourning, unable to speak. Toward evening he went up to the Temple and knelt before the altar. Raising his hands toward heaven he cried aloud.

"O my God, I am ashamed. I blush to lift my face toward You. After You have shown us so much kindness, more than we deserve, and let us return to our land, we are again breaking Your commandments. Behold, we have taken wives who serve strange gods and do all the shameful things forbidden by Your Torah. We stand guilty before You."

The people who had gathered about him wept bitterly.

"Trouble is sure to come of this," they whispered. "Remember what happened when King Ahab married Jezebel."

Then someone in the crowd cried aloud, "Ezra, you are a priest and a scribe. Set up a court and let those who have married the daughters of the Baal worshippers, divorce them."

It was hard to ask men to give up their wives. But Ezra saw no other way. If he did not act firmly, Judah would become like all the other nations. There would be no one to keep God's Torah. So Ezra set up courts throughout the land and those who had taken wives from the neighboring peoples divorced them.

Now, the neighbors grew more hostile to the Jews than ever. They attacked Jerusalem, set fire to the gates, and made breaks in the walls. Ezra was a great scholar and teacher, but he knew little about politics or fighting. For this, another kind of leader was needed. Such a leader was soon to come.

With Spade and Sword

In the land of Persia there lived a Jew named Nehemiah. Nehemiah held a high office in the court of the king. He was the king's trusted cup bearer.

One day a cousin of Nehemiah came to him from the land of Judah.

"Tell me how things are going in Jerusalem," Nehemiah asked eagerly.

The cousin answered, "Alas, they are going badly. Our enemies have broken down the wall and set fire to the gates. The people are in great misery."

Nehemiah was deeply disturbed by the news. All day he fasted, and prayed to God that he might find some way to help his people. Toward evening Nehemiah arose and went to the palace.

"Why do you look so sad, Nehemiah?" the king asked as Nehemiah handed him his wine. "You are not ill, so it must be some sorrow in your heart."

Nehemiah answered, "O king, live forever. Why should I not be sad when the city of my fathers lies in ruins?"

"Tell me what you wish me to do for you," the king said.

Nehemiah answered, "If it please the king, send me to Jerusalem, that I may rebuild it."

Then the king, and the queen who was sitting beside him, asked, "How long will you be away?"

When Nehemiah promised that he would surely return at a given time, the king agreed to let him go. He appointed Nehemiah governor of Judah, and gave him soldiers and horsemen to accompany him. So Nehemiah set out and arrived safely in Jerusalem.

Word spread quickly in Jerusalem that the king had sent a Jewish governor to rebuild its walls. Everyone offered to help, princes, merchants, carpenters, goldsmiths, farmers, the high priest himself.

At first their hostile neighbors looked on mockingly. "What are these Jews doing?" they asked. "Do they think they can build walls with burned stones out of the rubbish piles? If a fox should walk on their wall, it would break down."

But the walls rose steadily and gap after gap was filled in. Then the neighbors arose in rage and attacked Jerusalem from all sides.

Nehemiah strengthened the workers. Handing out swords and bows and spears, he said to them, "Do not be afraid of our enemies. Remember the Lord who is great and mighty, and fight for your families and your homes."

After this each man worked with a spade in one hand, and the other hand ready to draw the sword at his side.

Nehemiah, with his guard and a trumpeter, kept watch on the wall. He did not take off his clothes nor did his sword leave his hands by night or day.

When their enemies saw that the Jews were able to defend themselves, they thought up new schemes to stop the work.

A letter was sent to Nehemiah saying, "We know why you are building the city walls. It is because you are planning to rebel against the king. If you do not stop the work, we will report you to the king."

Nehemiah answered, "You have made all this up in your own heads." And he went on with the building until the walls of Jerusalem were completed.

Nehemiah Sees That Justice Is Done

Again Jerusalem was protected by strong walls. But Nehemiah's work was not yet done. The people had spent so much time rebuilding the walls, they had had to neglect their farms. Now the poor folk were without food or seed.

Nehemiah tried to make things as easy for the people as he could. He took no taxes from them as other governors did, although it was his duty to supply food for a hundred and fifty officers of the king. In addition he had to entertain ambassadors from other lands. It took an ox, six sheep, countless fowl, not to mention many jars of wine, to feed all these people for one day. Yet Nehemiah paid for it all out of his own pocket rather than tax the people. Besides this, he lent his poor neighbors money and grain.

But the other rich men were not like Nehemiah. Nehemiah heard bitter complaints as he went among the people.

One said, "We had to borrow money to buy bread. When we could not pay it back, our fields and our vineyards were taken from us."

Another said, "The king's tax came due. To pay it we borrowed money from our rich neighbors. Now they are taking our children away to be their servants."

Nehemiah was shocked.

He called an assembly of the rulers and spoke to them sternly.

"The thing you are doing is not good," he said. "I also lend the people money and grain, but I do not take away their belongings. Give the people back their sons and daughters, their fields and vineyards and olive groves."

The nobles did not dare to refuse.

They said to Nehemiah, "We will do as you say. We will give the people back all that we have taken."

"Swear!" Nehemiah said.

And they swore.

There were other evils which Nehemiah noticed. He stood near the gates of the city on the Sabbath and saw Jews buying and selling. Jewish farmers came in from the country. Their donkeys were laden with grain, wine, grapes, figs, vegetables. Nehemiah ordered the gate keepers to shut the gates of the city before the Sabbath began, and not to open them again until the Sabbath had passed.

After this the Sabbath was kept holy in Jerusalem.

The People Learn to Love the Torah

The time was drawing near for Nehemiah to return to Persia as he had promised the king and queen. The walls of Jerusalem were strong, the city safe. The people obeyed the laws of the Torah.

But Ezra knew that there was much more work to be done. It was not enough to obey God's laws because the governor commanded it. The people must keep the

Torah because they *wanted* to keep it. And they would *want* to keep it, only if they knew and understood it. He must teach the Torah to every man and woman and child in the land.

On Rosh Hashanah all the people, men and women and children, gathered in an open square. Ezra stood on a raised platform and read aloud from the Torah. From early morning to noon Nehemiah stood beside him. Ezra read, explaining each part, so that all the people might understand.

He read them God's promise to Abraham. *I will make of you a great nation. Through you all the nations of the earth shall be blessed.*

He told them of the days when they were slaves in Egypt and God saved them and brought them to Mount Sinai and gave them the Torah. He reminded them how God had watched over them in all their wanderings in the wilderness and given them this good land to be their home.

Then he read them God's laws.

Many of the people wept aloud, remembering how often they had been unfaithful to God. Ezra comforted them saying, "Do not weep. Rejoice, for this day is holy to our God."

As Sukkot drew near, Ezra sent the men into the mountains to cut green boughs for their *sukkot*. They returned, laden with wild olive and myrtle and palm. Each man built a *sukkah* for his family, on the roof of his house, or in his court, or in the open square. And there was joy and gladness for seven days.

After the holidays, the leaders of Judah, priests and levites and head of families, met with Ezra and Nehemiah. Faithfully they promised to make God's Torah the law of the land. An agreement was written and all who were present signed it.

After this Nehemiah returned to Persia, but Ezra stayed on.

All that he had done in Babylonia, Ezra now did in Jerusalem. His followers became teachers and faithful judges and scribes. With Ezra to help them, the scribes began to collect and make copies of all the writings of their people—the songs of David, the wise sayings of Solomon, the words of the prophets, the stories of the judges and the kings.

Nor was this all that Ezra did. He was a *Kohen* who loved the Holy Temple. But he saw that most people lived far from Jerusalem. They came up to the Temple only on Pesach and Shavuot and Sukkot.

Ezra said, "It is not enough to worship God three times a year. Sacrifices may be offered only in the Temple, but we can study and pray wherever we live. Let us meet for prayer and study on Sabbaths and market days."

This the people did. The houses where they met were called synagogues. To the synagogues they came to pray and give thanks to God. On Sabbaths, and on Mondays and Thursdays when the farmers came to town, they read out of the Torah. From this time on Jews no longer *wanted* to serve false gods. They had come to love God and his Torah.

The people said, "Since Moses there has been no teacher like Ezra the scribe."

The Story of Esther

The Maiden Named Hadassah

HAVE YOU EVER seen the myrtle, the tree that is called in Hebrew *hadas* or *haddasah*? It is beautiful by day and even lovelier when darkness falls. Then its leaves fill the air with fragrance and its pure white blossoms shine like stars.

Once in the land of Persia there lived a gentle Jewish maiden, an orphan who had been raised by her good cousin Mordecai. Her name was Hadassah and she had the beauty of the *haddasim*. In Persian, the maiden was called Esther.

It happened at this time that Ahasuerus, king of Persia, made a great feast for all the princes and the rulers of his kingdom. They gathered together in Shushan, the capital. This was the city where Mordecai and Esther lived.

Never had there been so splendid a banquet. It was held in the open court of the palace. The pavement was of many colored marble, green and white and black. Rare blue and white hangings were fastened to marble pillars. The guests reclined on couches of gold and silver, and drank out of cups of gold.

Inside the palace Vashti, the queen, held a banquet for the wives of the princes. In Persia it was not considered modest for a woman to attend a feast along with the men.

On the seventh day, when the heart of the king was merry with wine, he ordered Vashti to appear before him so that all might see her beauty. But Vashti refused to come.

Then the king was highly angered and said to the princes, "What shall be done to Queen Vashti who refuses to obey my commands?"

The princes answered, "Queen Vashti has wronged not only the king, but all the men of the kingdom. When the women hear what the queen has done, they too will refuse to obey their husbands. If it please the king, let the crown be taken from Queen Vashti and given to another who is better than she."

King Ahasuerus, who was a mighty king but not a very wise one, took the advice of the princes. Messengers were appointed to search through all the lands in the kingdom for beautiful maidens to be brought before the king. The maiden who pleased the king best would become queen in Vashti's place.

When Esther heard of the royal decree she would not leave her room for fear that the messengers of the king would find her and take her to the place. But Esther's beauty was too well known. One day the messengers of the king knocked at Mordecai's door, and Esther was led away to the palace.

Esther Becomes Queen

Beautiful maidens from every part of the kingdom had been gathered in the Women's House of the palace. Esther was the last to be brought in.

The maidens stared at her and whispered to one another:

"She is certainly not stately," said the tall, blue-eyed princess from the north.

"Nor delicately small," said the little black-eyed princess from the south. "She is just average."

"And her color! It is almost sallow," said the maiden with the rose-petal skin.

All this was true. Yet there was a grace and charm in Esther that drew people toward her. The servants loved her. The keeper of the Women's House was eager to serve her.

For twelve months the maidens remained in the House of the Women, beautifying themselves with fragrant oils and perfumes, as was the custom.

When the twelve months drew to an end, the keeper of the Women's House called the maidens together and said to them, "All the treasures of the palace are yours to choose from. Name whatever you wish, either to wear or to take with you when you go before the king, and it shall be given you."

The maidens asked for rare silks, embroidered veils, for shawls as finely spun as cobwebs, for charms and jewels—diamonds, pearls, rubies, sapphires. The little dark-eyed princess ordered a gown made of hummingbird feathers. The maiden with the rose-petal skin insisted on coal black slaves to go before her.

One by one the maidens came into the king's presence each one dazzling in beauty, wondrously attired. Esther alone had asked for nothing. She stood before the king, gentle and modest, wearing a simple white gown.

And King Ahasuerus chose Esther from among all the maidens. He placed the crown upon her head and made her queen.

Haman Plots Against the Jews

Each day Mordecai sat at the king's gate so that he might be near if Esther needed him. No one in the palace knew that he was related to the queen, for he had bidden Esther not to speak about her family. There were people in the court who were hostile to the Jews and Mordecai feared that they might do Esther harm if they learned that she was a Jewess.

One day, as Mordecai sat at the gate, he overheard two officers of the court plotting to kill the king. They spoke a language which was not known in Shushan. But Mordecai had studied the languages of all the seventy nations of the world and understood what they said. He sent word of the plot to Esther who reported it to the king. The charge was looked into, found to be true, and the plotters were put to death.

Soon after this, King Ahasuerus promoted a certain proud and haughty man named Haman to the highest office in the land. It was Haman's delight, as he passed through the king's gate, to see the people bow to the ground before him. Mordecai alone did not bow.

"Why do you not bow before Haman?" the king's servants asked Mordecai.

Mordecai answered, "I am a Jew and bow to the ground only before God."

When Haman heard of Mordecai's answer he was filled with rage. It was not enough for him to punish Mordecai alone. He made up his mind to destroy Mordecai's entire people, all the Jews in the kingdom.

So he went to King Ahasuerus and said to him, "There is a certain people scattered through your kingdom whose laws are different from the laws of every other people. They do not obey the laws of the king. If it pleases the king, let this people be destroyed and I will pay ten thousand talents of silver into your treasury."

King Ahasuerus—who was a mighty king but certainly not a wise one—did not stop to see if Haman's words were true, but said to Haman, "The Jews are yours. Do with them whatever you think best."

At once Haman had the king's scribe write out a decree. The decree said that on the fourteenth day of the month of Adar all the Jews in the kingdom, men and women, children and infants were to be slain. Not one was to be left alive. The decree was signed with the king's seal, and messengers were sent out to carry it to every part of the kingdom.

Mordecai was sitting at the king's gate when the messengers came out of the palace. Stunned by the dreadful news, he set out for home. On the way he met three children returning from school.

"What verse did you learn today?" Mordecai asked them, for the school children memorized a Bible verse each day.

The first boy answered, "Do not be afraid of sudden fear nor of the trouble brought by the wicked."

The second one recited, "Let them plot together but the plot will fail, for God is with us."

The third boy said, "My verse was, 'I, the Lord, created you. Yes, and I will save you.'"

When Mordecai heard these words spoken by the children, he was ashamed that he had so quickly given up hope.

He sent words of hope to the Jews of Shushan, who, weeping and wailing, had shut themselves into their homes.

"Fast and pray to God," Mordecai said to them. Then he put on mourning clothes, sack cloth and ashes, and went out into the streets as far as the palace gates.

Now Esther had not yet heard of the decree against the Jews. She was in her chambers when a trusted servant came to her, saying, "Your cousin Mordecai is standing in front of the palace, clothed in sack cloth."

Esther was deeply distressed.

"Go quickly and ask him what this means," she said. "Why has he come to the palace in sack cloth?"

The servant soon returned with a copy of the decree and a request from Mordecai, "Esther, go to the king and plead for your people's life."

But it was the law in Persia that no one, not even the queen, was permitted to go before the king unless she had been asked to do so. This was known to everyone in the land.

Esther said to the servant, "Tell my cousin Mordecai that I have not been called by the king for thirty days. If I go before him uninvited, the guards will put me to death—unless the king should save me by holding out his scepter."

Mordecai answered Esther, "Do not think you will escape the fate of your people even in the royal palace. If you keep silent, help will come to the Jews in another way, but you and your family will perish. Who knows whether you were not made queen for just such a time as this."

This time Esther answered Mordecai, "Go! Gather together all the Jews in Shushan, and bid them fast and pray for me. I and my maidens will also fast. Then will I go before the king. And if I perish, I perish."

Esther Saves Her People

King Ahasuerus sat on his royal throne with his courtiers around him. Suddenly all eyes turned toward the open court. Queen Esther, dressed in her royal robes and attended by her maids, stood in the entrance. The guards drew their swords, but she paid no heed. Never had she seemed so beautiful to the king. He held out his scepter and she drew near and touched it. The guards returned their swords to their sheaths.

Then the king said to Esther, "What is your wish Queen Esther? It shall be given you even to the half of my kingdom."

Esther answered, "If it please the king, let the king and Haman come this day to a banquet I have prepared for them."

Then she turned and left the court.

So the king and Haman came to Esther's banquet.

Again the king asked, "What is your wish, Queen Esther? It shall be granted, even to the half of my kingdom."

Again Esther answered, "If I have pleased the king, let the king and Haman banquet with me tomorrow."

Haman left Esther's palace joyful and glad of heart. But when he passed Mordecai at the king's gate and Mordecai neither arose nor bowed, Haman was filled with rage. He hurried home to his wife Zeresh and his ten sons and said to them, "Not only has the king given me glory and riches and promoted me above all the princes, but today the queen invited me to a banquet. Yet I cannot enjoy my good fortune so long as I see the Jew Mordecai sitting in the king's gate."

Then Zeresh, Haman's wife, said to him, "Let a gallows be made, seventy-five feet high. In the morning ask the king to have Mordecai hanged on it."

"Your advice pleases me," Haman said, and he hurried out to have the gallows built.

That night the king tossed restlessly and could not sleep. He asked his servant to read to him from the book of records, and it happened that the servant came to the account of the plot against the king—how Mordecai discovered the plot and saved the king's life.

"What honors have been given to this Mordecai?" King Ahasuerus asked.

"Nothing has been done for him," the servant answered.

At this the king was greatly disturbed.

Now Haman had been waiting outside the king's door since sunrise, so eager was he to get permission to have Mordecai hanged. The king noticed that someone was outside, and asked, "Who is in the court?"

The servant answered, "Haman is outside."

"Let him enter," the king said.

Haman was called in, and the king said to him, "Tell me, Haman, what shall be done to the man whom the king delights to honor?"

Haman was greatly pleased, for he thought, "Whom would the king delight to honor but me?"

He answered, "Let the man be clothed in the king's royal robes, and let him ride on the king's own horse, the horse that wears a crown upon its head. Let one of the noblest of the princes go before him proclaiming, 'Thus shall be done to the man whom the king delights to honor.' "

The king said, "Make haste Haman. Take the garments and the horse and do as you have said to Mordecai the Jew."

There was nothing Haman could do about it. He had to clothe Mordecai in royal robes, seat him on the king's own horse and lead him through the streets of the city crying aloud, "Thus shall be done to the man whom the king delights to honor."

The people looked on, amazed.

After this Mordecai returned to the king's gate.

Haman hurried home, with his head bowed. He told his wife Zeresh what had happened, hoping that she would comfort him.

But Zeresh said, "Now that you have begun to fall before Mordecai, you will keep on falling."

They were still talking when the king's servant came in, and Haman had to hurry to the queen's banquet.

At the queen's feast the king asked again, "What is your petition, Queen Esther? It shall be given to you even to the half of my kingdom."

This time Esther answered, "O my King, if I have found favor in your eyes, let my life be spared and the life of my people. For we have been sold, I and my people, to be destroyed, to be slain, to perish."

The king looked at Esther in amazement.

"Who is he—where is he—who dared to do this?"

Esther pointed to Haman, "An enemy—this wicked Haman."

Terrified, Haman threw himself at the queen's feet begging for his life.

The king arose in great anger and had Haman seized.

Then the Keeper of the Palace came forward and said, "There are gallows seventy-five feet high which Haman prepared for Mordecai."

"Hang Haman on them," the king commanded.

Thus the Jews were saved. Swift messengers carried the good news to every part of the kingdom, and the Jews of Persia rejoiced and gave thanks to God.

This is how the fourteenth day of Adar was changed from sorrow to gladness. Esther asked that the day be made a holiday, the joyful festival of Purim, a day of feasting and merriment, of sending gifts to one another, and gifts to the poor.

The Story of Judah Maccabee

Antiochus the Madman

IN THE HILL TOWN of Modin, north of Jerusalem, there once lived five brothers, all brave, sturdy youths, faithful to God. Their father was the good priest Mattathias. The strongest and the bravest of the five was named Judah. Once Judah asked his father why he never went up to Jerusalem to serve in the Temple.

The eyes of Mattathias flashed with anger, as he answered, "Because the high priest is not worthy of his office. It was King Antiochus who made him high priest in return for a promise of gold."

King Antiochus was not a Jewish king. He was a Syrian whose armies had won him a great empire. Judea was but one of the nations over which he ruled.

Antiochus called himself Antiochus the magnificent. People called him Antiochus the madman. He had copied the ways of Greece, as was the fashion at this time, and he wanted to make Greeks of all the people in his kingdom.

So he sent out a letter saying, "Let every nation give up its religion and its laws so that we may be one people."

Most of the nations found it easy to obey the king's command. They served so many gods, it made no difference to them if they added a few more.

But Jews like Mattathias and his sons said, "Shall we who pray to the one God bow down before idols?" And they kept their laws more strictly than ever.

Judah had heard that even among the Jews, there were some who obeyed the king's command. They said, "Our Jewish ways are old-fashioned. Everybody of importance has turned Greek."

Instead of studying Torah, they spent all their time in Greek gymnasiums, exercising and wrestling and watching games held in honor of the Greek gods.

"It does not matter," they said, "if we make an offering to an image now and then."

Once Judah went up to Jerusalem to bring a message to his father's old friend, Eleazar the scribe. There he saw some of these Jews hurrying by on their way to the games. They dressed like Greeks, spoke in Greek, called one another by Greek names. In the gymnasiums they tried to keep their Greek neighbors from knowing they were Jews. Judah despised them. He was glad to get back to his home in Modin.

For the Holy Laws

Scarcely had Judah returned to Modin when dreadful news came from Jerusalem. The mad Antiochus had set up an image of Zeus in the Holy Temple. Pigs were sacrificed on the altar. Antiochus was determined to make an end of the Jewish religion. His soldiers were everywhere. Was a man found reading in the holy books? Honoring the Sabbath? Keeping any of the laws of the Torah? He was put to death.

Refugees began passing through Modin. They were on their way to the mountains where they hoped to hide out in caves. Mattathias hid them by day and sent them on after dark, guided by his sons; for Judah and his brothers knew every path in the wilderness.

The fleeing people had terrible stories to tell. From them Mattathias learned what had happened to his friend, Eleazer. The ninety year old scribe was dragged to a wicked feast. Pig's meat was forced into his mouth. He spat it out. Even the cruel soldiers pitied the old man.

They said to him, "Tomorrow bring your own meat to the feast, such as you are permitted to eat. Then you need only pretend to eat the meat of the sacrifice. In this way we can save you from death."

But Eleazar answered, "If I pretend to eat, many young persons will think that Eleazar, a man of ninety years, has gone over to a strange religion. Shall I, in order to live a little longer, mislead them? Nay, I will go to my death. Thus will I leave a proper example to the young that they may die willingly and bravely for the holy laws."

The young men did follow Eleazar's example. There were the seven sons of the widow Hannah. Together with their mother, they were brought before the king.

He commanded them, "Bow before my gods and eat the flesh of the sacrifice."

The eldest answered, "We are ready to die rather than break the laws of our fathers."

The king fell into a rage and had the young man put to death with dreadful tortures.

The second son was ordered to bow before the image.

He answered, "My brother bowed not, neither will I."

And they did to him as they had done to the first.

So one by one the sons of Hannah went bravely to their death, until only the youngest was left. He was no more than a child.

"You are too young to die," the king said to him. "See, I will drop my ring upon the ground. Only bow and pick it up so that you *seem* to be bowing to my gods, and I will spare your life."

But the boy stood straighter than before.

The king turned to the mother. "Speak to your son," he said. "Bid him save his life."

"I will speak to him," the mother answered. Then she said to the boy, "O my son, do not fear this tormentor, and be worthy of your brothers."

The boy looked up at the king. "Why are you waiting?" he asked. "I will not break the commandments of our God."

Then the cruel tyrant sent this one also to his death.

Last, after all her sons, the mother died.

When Judah heard what had been done to Hannah's sons, he cried out to his brothers, "How long shall we wait here doing nothing? Let us go up to Jerusalem and fight for our people and our holy laws."

But Simon, his elder brother, said, "In Jerusalem one can only *die* for the law. Let us *live* for it. Be patient, Judah. The tyrant is sending his soldiers from town to town to force the people to sacrifice to his gods. When they come to Modin, we shall know what to do."

Whoever Is for the Lord, Follow Me

The soldiers of King Antiochus came to Modin, as Simon had said. An altar and an image of Zeus were set up in the public square, and all the townspeople were ordered to gather there. Mattathias and his five sons were among them.

The officer of the king turned to Mattathias.

"You are a leader in this town," he said. "Come and be the first to fulfill the king's command, as all the nations have done. Then you and your family will be rewarded with riches and honor."

Mattathias answered in a voice loud enough for all to hear. "Though all the other nations obey the king and turn away from their religion, yet will I and my sons

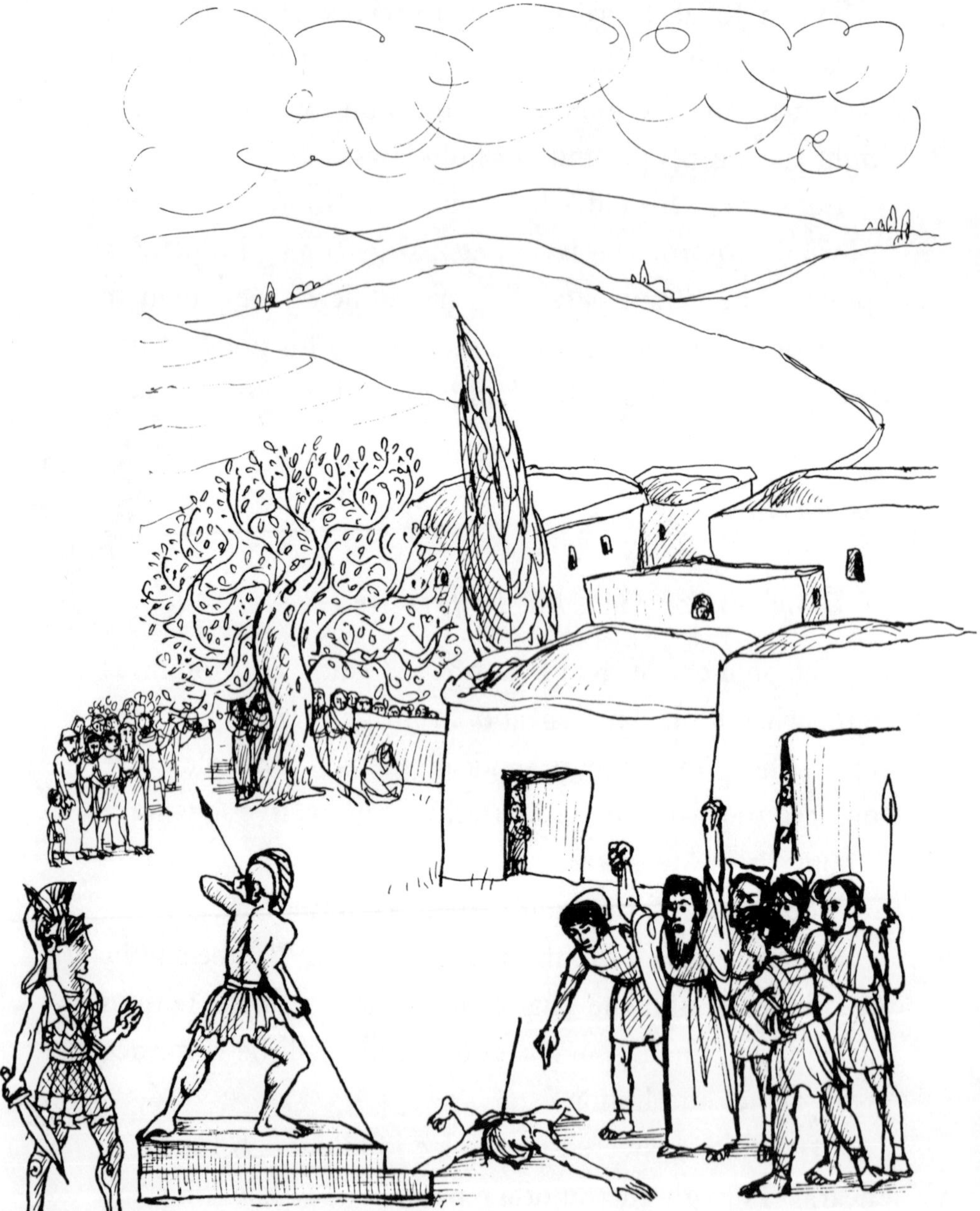

follow in the way of our fathers. We will not turn from our religion either on the right hand or on the left."

Scarcely had he spoken, when a cowardly Jew, dressed in Greek clothes, stepped up to the altar. He lifted the knife, ready to make the sacrifice. Mattathias trembled with anger. Rushing forward, he struck the traitor down. Then he turned on the king's officer and killed him, too. Quickly, his sons surrounded him.

Mattathias cried aloud, "Whoever is for the Lord, follow me."

Then he and his sons fled into the mountains, leaving all that they owned behind. Many brave men joined them, bringing with them their wives and children and their cattle. Like other Jewish bands, they found shelter in the caves that reached deep into the mountains. At night they came forth and went about the countryside. They broke down the Greek altars. They attacked the soldiers sent to enforce the king's commands. Thus many Jews were saved.

Before Mattathias died, he called his sons to his side and said to them, "My sons, your brother Simon is a man of wisdom. He shall be a father to you. But let Judah be your captain and lead you in battle."

Then he blessed them and bade them fight bravely for their people and the Torah.

The Few Against the Many

Now that Judah was the leader, the attacks against the Syrians grew bolder. To get weapons for his men, Judah would appear suddenly in a Syrian camp, strike down the guards, seize their shields and spears and swords, then disappear in the hills. The hired soldiers of Antiochus were in terror of him. The Jews took heart.

"Maccabee is a fitting name for Judah," they said. "He is a *maccab*, a hard hitting hammer."

People said that Judah was a lion in courage. Each day new recruits joined him. Among them were some of the Jews who had tried to become Greeks. Now, shocked by the cruelty of Antiochus, they were coming back to their own people.

Word reached the Syrian general that a ragged band of rebels were daring to defy the king. He said, "I will force them out of their hiding places."

With a large army, he set out for the hills. But Judah did not wait for the Syrians to reach him. He went to meet them. The Syrian army was routed and their general killed. Judah used the sword of this general for the rest of his life.

A second general with a second army set out. This time Judah lay in wait for him above a rocky pass that led up from the plain. From their hiding place, Judah's men could see the Syrian army begin the long climb.

They said to Judah, "How can we who are so few fight against this vast army?"

Judah answered, "With God it does not matter whether there are many or few. They come against us with wickedness and pride to destroy us and our wives and little ones. But we fight for our lives and our Torah."

As he spoke, Judah gave the signal to attack. His men leaped upon the Syrians winding through the narrow pass. Again Judah was successful. The second army and the second general were defeated.

King Antiochus was furious when he learned what had happened to his generals. This time he himself sent out an army. There were footmen and horse men and fighting elephants with *two* generals in charge. Slave dealers followed, with bags of gold and silver, sure that there would be great numbers of Jewish captives to buy up.

At Mizpah, where Samuel the prophet had once lived, Judah and his men gathered to fast and pray. Judah unrolled a *Sefer Torah* which he had rescued. On it the mocking heathens had scrawled images of their gods. When Judah's soldiers saw it they cried out in grief.

"O God," they prayed, "You alone are our help."

In the camp of the Syrians, the generals of Antiochus were making their plans. They would surprise Judah that very night before he had time to surprise them. As soon as darkness fell, half the Syrian army set out and arrived at Judah's camp. The camp fires were still burning but Judah and his men had gone.

"They have fled in fear of us," the general said, and pressed on in pursuit, further and further into the mountains. But Judah had not fled. He had gotten word of the Syrian plan. At that very moment he was leading his army by another route to the Syrian camp. His men were few in number, many of them without shields or swords. But Judah put faith and courage in them all.

"Fear not the enemy's numbers," he said to them. "Remember how our fathers were saved when Pharaoh pursued them."

Dawn was breaking. In the Syrian camp the soldiers lay fast asleep. Suddenly a blare of trumpets awakened them—strange trumpets. They looked about them, bewildered. Tents were burning, swords flashing. They heard shouts in Hebrew. All around them men were falling. The Judeans, whom their general had gone to destroy, were here in their camp. Panic took hold of the soldiers and they fled, pursued by Judah's men.

Again the trumpet sounded. Judah was giving his troops new orders.

"Stand ready! The rest of the Syrian army will soon return from the mountains. They will be weary from their fool's errand. But anger will lend them strength."

Even as he spoke the Syrians appeared on the hill top. But there was no second battle that day. The hired soldiers of Antiochus saw the smoke rising from their burning tents. They saw the Judeans, whom they had pursued all day, waiting in their own camp to do battle with them. And they turned and fled in terror all the way to the land of the Philistines.

The camp was strewn with badly needed weapons, shields and helmets, swords and spears. Judah's men gathered them up. The gold and silver, dropped by the slave dealers, was divided carefully, half for the fighters, half for the widows and the orphans.

After this, Judah and his men returned to their camp and gave thanks to God.

And the Light Did Not Go Out

Three years had passed since Antiochus had seized the holy Temple. The way to Jerusalem was open at last. Judah lost no time. His army marched into the city, through the silent streets, up Mount Zion to the Temple. There they stood, aghast. The Temple was deserted. Its gates were burned down. The courts, where joyous crowds had gathered, were overgrown with weeds. Pigs' blood was spattered on the altar and on the stairs.

The soldiers knelt with their faces to the ground and mourned, but the sound of trumpets soon roused them. Judah was giving orders. Half the army was to stand guard against attack. The rest were to help the priests repair and cleanse the Temple. Eagerly they set to work, clearing the courts, rebuilding the walls and gates. The altar had been made unclean by the sacrifice of pigs. Faithful priests, who had fought along with Judah, pulled it down and built a new altar in its place. They purified the Holy of Holies, hung up the veils, prepared a new menorah for the *Ner Tamid*, the eternal light.

On the twenty-fifth day of the month of *Kislev*, the work was completed.

Joyous crowds gathered in the Temple courts to see the *Ner Tamid* relit. But the priests delayed.

A whisper ran through the crowd, "There is no fit oil for the lamp. The heathens have made all the oil impure."

Feverishly the priests hunted in every room and hiding place. One jar of oil was found at last. They knew that it was pure, for it was still sealed with the seal of the high priest. But the jar was small. It contained only enough oil to last one day. Nevertheless, they poured the oil into the lamp and kindled the light. And a great wonder happened. *The light did not go out.* Eight days that little light burned. By then new oil had been prepared.

Judah and his men marched joyously around the altar. Throughout the land there was gladness and thanksgiving.

But the struggle was not yet over. Hard battles still remained to be fought. In one of these battles Judah met his death, but his brothers fought on. In the end the Syrians were driven out of the land. The fathers and mothers and children who had fled to the mountains returned to their homes. Again the Jews were free to keep the Sabbath, study in the holy books, and obey the laws of the Torah.

On Ḥanukah we kindle lights in remembrance of those days. Then we think of Judah Maccabee, his father and his brothers, who were the first to fight for the liberty to worship God as they thought right.

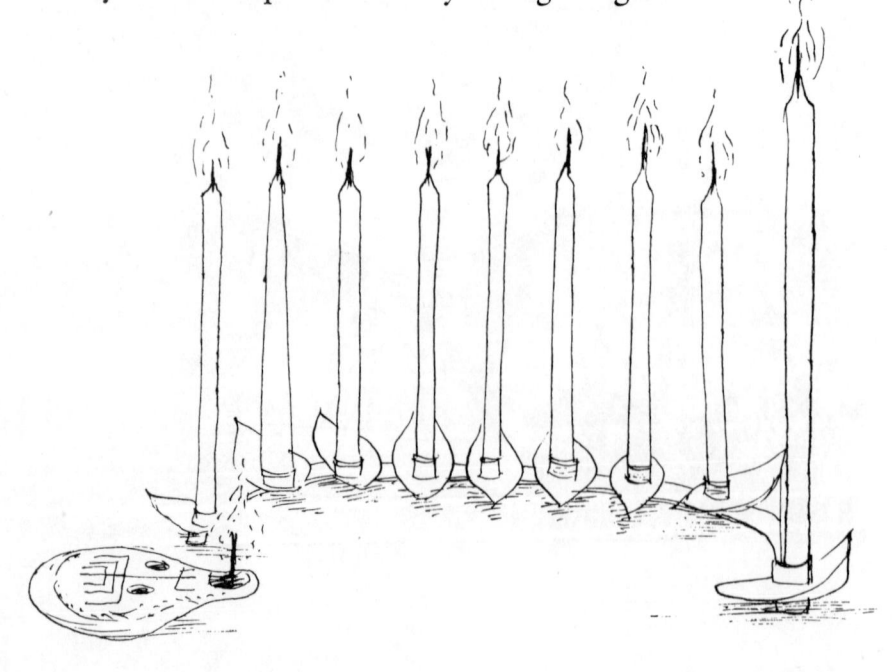

Rabbis and Teachers

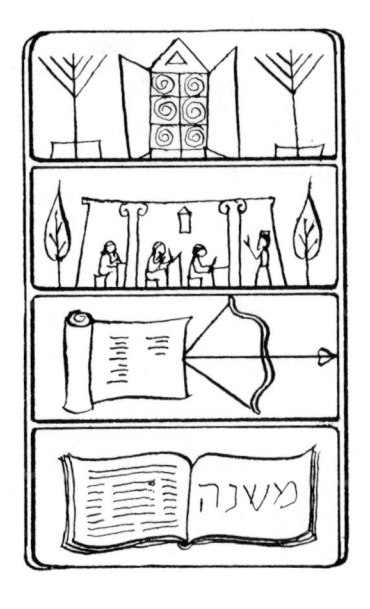

HILLEL

JOHANAN BEN ZAKKAI

AKIBA

JUDAH THE PRINCE

The Story of Hillel

On the Schoolhouse Roof

FROM THE DAYS of Ezra, there had always been important schools of Torah in Jerusalem. They were called Houses of Study or academies.

It happened one Sabbath that snow fell during the night. This was unusual in Jerusalem. By Sabbath morning the flat roofs were covered with snow. Inside the schoolhouse the rabbis sat studying.

Said one rabbi to the other, "What makes the room so dark? It is always light by this time."

They looked up at the skylight. A dark form lay across it, covered with snow. Quickly the rabbis hurried out of doors, up a ladder to the roof. They brushed the snow away. A youth was lying there, unconscious and numb with cold.

"It is the lad who listens so intently to our lectures," the first rabbi said. "The one from Babylonia."

Anxiously, the rabbis carried the youth into the house. Though all work was forbidden on the Sabbath, they warmed oil over the fire and rubbed him gently until he stirred and opened his eyes. He looked up at them questioningly.

"We found you on the skylight covered with snow," the rabbis explained. "How did you come to be on the roof?"

The lad stammered out his story. His name was Hillel. He was a Babylonian. He had come to Jerusalem to study Torah. To earn his living he chopped wood, earning a few coins each day. Half the coins went for food and lodging. The other half, he paid to the doorkeeper of the school. But the day before he had been unable to earn any money at all, and the doorkeeper had turned him away.

The youth hesitated, then went on with his story:

"My masters, I longed to hear your words. They are the words of the living God. I swung myself up to the roof and listened at the skylight. It was cold and I was tired. I must have fallen asleep and snow covered me."

He looked at the basin of oil warming on the fire and said in distress, "Because of me you have broken the Sabbath."

The rabbis answered, "To save a life one is permitted to break the Sabbath. It was worth breaking it for one like you, Hillel."

After this the rabbis told the doorkeeper he was always to admit Hillel without charge.

Now Hillel could spend more time than ever on his studies. There was much to learn, all the laws that were written down in the Torah, and many laws and teachings that had not been written down. Hillel stored away in his memory every word his teachers taught. By the time he returned to Babylonia he knew the whole Torah by heart.

Many years passed and Hillel came again to Jerusalem. By this time he had a wife and children. It was just before Passover. Jews from many lands had come up to celebrate the festival in the Temple. They came from all parts of Judea and from distant lands, from Babylonia and Egypt, from Greece and Rome. The city was crowded with joyful pilgrims.

But in the schools, the scholars sat troubled. A question had been asked which no one could answer. It had to do with the proper way to celebrate the Passover. The great rabbis who had been Hillel's teachers had died, and there were new teachers in the schools. Neither the teachers nor any of the scholars remembered this law. One scholar said this and another scholar said that. Passover was coming, and no one knew what to tell the people.

Then someone said, "There is a man in Jerusalem, Hillel the Babylonian, who once studied under our great teachers. Perhaps he can help us."

So Hillel was sent for.

At once he gave the answer to the question.

Then the rabbis who were at the head of the school arose from their seats and said, "Hillel is a greater scholar than we are. He is more worthy to be your teacher than we."

They insisted on giving up their place and making Hillel the head of the school.

A Wager Is Lost

In the Temple in Jerusalem there was a great stone hall. In the hall sat seventy scholars and priests, the judges and the law makers of the land. The assembly was called the *Sanhedrin*. At its head sat two honored rabbis, Hillel and Shammai.

Like Hillel, Shammai was a scholar and a teacher. He loved God and wanted everyone to keep the Torah. But in all other ways Hillel and Shammai were different.

"Greet everyone cheerfully," Shammai would say, but he had a quick temper and found it hard to do as he taught. Hillel was always gentle and patient. One day a man made a bet that he could get Hillel angry. He bet four hundred *zuzim*, which was a large sum of money in those days.

On a Friday afternoon when Hillel was preparing for the Sabbath, the young man walked past his house.

"Hillel!" he shouted. "Where is Hillel?"

Hillel, who was bathing himself, wrapped a robe around him, and hurried to the door.

"I am Hillel," he said. "What is it you wish, my son?"

"I have a question to ask you," said the man.

"Ask," said Hillel.

"Why do the Babylonians have queerly shaped heads?" the man asked.

He meant this as an insult, knowing that Hillel was a Babylonian.

But Hillel answered quietly, "That is a good question. The reason is that they have no skilled women to look after the infants when they are born."

The man went off, but in a few moments he was back. Hillel had just returned to his bath when he heard him shouting. "Hillel! Where is Hillel?"

Once more Hillel wrapped himself in a robe and went to the door.

"I have another question to ask," said the man.

"Ask, my son," said Hillel.

"Why do the people of Tadmon have weak eyes?" asked the man.

"That too, is a good question," said Hillel. "It is because they live in a sandy country. The wind drives sand into their eyes."

The man turned away, discouraged, but soon tried again.

"Hillel! Where is Hillel?" he shouted.

A third time Hillel interrupted his bath to go to the door.

"What is it you wish now, my son?"

"I want to know why the Africans have broad feet," said the man.

Hillel answered, "They need broad feet to tramp over the marshy land."

The man made a last effort to win his bet.

"Are you the Hillel who is the head of the Sanhedrin?" he asked.

"I am," said Hillel.

"If you are the one, may there be no more like you in Israel!" the man shouted angrily.

But Hillel was not to be provoked.

"Why do you say this?" he asked.

"Because on your account I have lost four hundred *zuzim*."

Then he told Hillel the story of the wager.

Hillel laughed and said, "If this has taught you not to make foolish bets, the money is not lost. Better that you should lose twice four hundred *zuzim* than that Hillel should lose his temper."

Hillel Says—Shammai Says

In school and outside of school the pupils of Shammai would argue with the pupils of Hillel. One day a bricklayer was sitting high up on a scaffold. In the middle of his work, he put down his bricks and began to pray.

"*Shema Yisrael———*"

One of Shammai's pupils happened to be passing.

He called up to the bricklayer, "That is no way to recite the *Shema*. You should have said it before you left for work."

The man looked down and answered, "When I left for work it was still dark. Could I recite the morning *Shema* before morning?"

A number of passersby had stopped to listen. Shammai's pupil turned to them.

"That ignorant bricklayer does not know how to pray," he said. "In the evening one must recite the *Shema*

while lying down, in the morning, standing up. So Shammai says."

"That is not what Hillel says," said a young farm worker. He was leading a donkey loaded with fruit. "I myself asked Hillel about this. I said to him, 'How am I to say the morning *Shema?* Sometimes my work begins before daybreak.'

"Hillel answered me, 'It does not matter where or how you say the *Shema*. The important thing is to say it. If you are picking fruit and the time comes to pray, put down your basket and pray right there in the tree.' "

Other workmen nodded their heads approvingly.

"We agree with Hillel," they said. "Hillel understands us. He was a woodchopper himself."

All sorts of people felt that Hillel understood them—brides, for instance!

In those days it was the custom for wedding guests to dance before the bride and sing her praises.

"The bride is gentle and modest. She is beautiful to behold."

One day in the school someone asked the question, "Suppose the bride is not beautiful? Is it right to call her beautiful?"

Shammai answered, "It is not right. One must describe the bride exactly as she is."

170

But Hillel smiled and said, "Every bride should be called beautiful on her wedding day."

The rest of the scholars agreed with Hillel.

"Is there a bride who is not beautiful on her wedding day?" one of them asked. "Happiness makes her beautiful."

The people followed Hillel's rule and all the brides were made happy.

If You Were He

More and more men, young and old, flocked to Hillel's school.

Shammai would say, "Only good men of good families, who can spend all their time in study should be admitted to the schools."

So he had few pupils, most of them rich men's sons.

But Hillel welcomed everyone, young and old, rich and poor, even sinners. He would say, "A wrongdoer who listens to the Torah may turn from his evil ways. I have known some of them to become the parents of good and holy men."

Many of his pupils came to school after a hard day's work. But Hillel could keep the most tired student awake. Sometimes it was a good story that stirred their interest. Sometimes Hillel would crowd many thoughts into a few words as one does in a riddle, and would let his pupils puzzle out his meaning.

Even after school, Hillel's students would follow him about. They said, "We can learn as much from watching Hillel as from listening to him. Whatever he teaches others to do he does himself."

This was so.

Hillel would say, "Do not judge a man until you have been in his place."

One of his pupils asked, "What if we *must* judge a man and we haven't been in his place?"

Hillel answered, "Imagine yourself in his place. Try to think how you would feel, if you were he."

This was just what Hillel did.

Once a rich man suddenly lost his wealth. All his life he had helped others. Now, in his old age, he himself was in need. As soon as Hillel heard of this he had his wife send food to the man, vegetables and bread.

But the next day Hillel began thinking, "To me bread and turnips make a good meal. But this man has been used to meat and fish and fowl. It must be hard for him to have nothing to eat but bread and vegetables."

"My wife," he said, "see that meat is sent to the man along with the vegetables."

A few days later Hillel met the man trudging slowly along the street.

Again Hillel began thinking, "If I had ridden a horse all my life, would it not be hard to go on foot in my old age?"

He had a horse sent to the old man. Later he sent a servant to look after him.

One of the neighbor women spoke to Hillel's wife about this.

"Why do you let your husband send this poor man such luxuries? A horse and a servant, indeed!"

Hillel's wife answered, "To you and me a horse and servant are luxuries. But to an old man who has been used to them all his life, they are not luxuries. My husband is right."

Once the tables were turned and it was Hillel who said, "My wife is right."

It happened one day when Hillel brought a guest home to dinner. Hillel and his guest sat down at the table. A half hour passed, and no food was brought in. Another half hour passed. Still no food! Yet Hillel had told his wife he was bringing home a guest. At last his wife entered and set the meal before them.

"My wife," Hillel asked, "what makes you so late?"

She flushed and said, "I am sorry I kept you wait-

173

ing. The meal was ready, but just as I was going to serve it a poor man came to the door. He was bringing home a bride but had no food in the house for a wedding meal. So I gave him our dinner and had to begin cooking all over again."

Hillel said to her, "You did right, my wife. A person in need must be helped at once—and this was a bridegroom on his wedding day. All that you do is out of loving kindness."

Both Speak God's Words

Hillel was gentle and patient. Shammai was strict and quick tempered. But Shammai, too, loved God with all his heart. No one went to more trouble to keep every law of the Torah than Shammai.

Once his daughter-in-law gave birth to a son during the week of Sukkot. Shammai was overjoyed.

He said, "Now my grandson need not wait until he is eight days old to keep a commandment of God. He can perform a *mitzvah* at once."

"What *mitzvah*, father?" his son asked.

"What *mitzvah* do you suppose? The *mitzvah* of sitting in the *sukkah!*" Shammai answered.

"But, father, the baby is too young to be taken into the *sukkah*."

"Then we will bring the *sukkah* to him," Shammai said.

He had an opening cut into the roof over the bed where the baby was lying, and covered it with branches.

Shammai's pupils were few, but they were loyal to their master, always ready to defend him. They liked to repeat the good advice he gave.

"Speak little and do much."

"Set aside a regular time to study Torah."

They insisted that Shammai's way of explaining the Torah was the only proper way. Shammai said that the important thing was to keep the Torah strictly, the stricter the better. If there happened to be an easier way and a harder way to keep a law, he chose the harder way.

Hillel said, "God gave the Torah for the sake of His children. One must not ask, 'Which way is easier?' 'Which way is harder?' but 'Which way will make life better?'"

Even the people who agreed with Hillel, considered Shammai a great and good man.

They said, "Hillel speaks the words of the living God, and Shammai speaks the words of the living God."

They remembered the teachings of both rabbis and taught them to their children. But in the end Hillel's teachings became the law.

The Whole Torah

Hillel lived to a good old age, beloved by everyone. When he died the whole people mourned him, calling him the gentle one, the modest one, the follower of Ezra.

Even after his death people told stories about him.

One day three men sat talking together when a little boy ran up to them.

"This is my son, Hillel," said the first man.

Said the second, "May your young Hillel grow up as gentle and wise as the elder Hillel."

Then the third man spoke, "If the lad is like the elder Hillel he will be blessed indeed. The impatience of Shammai almost drove me from God's teachings but the patience of Hillel drew me near."

Then he told them this story.

"I was not born a Jew. One day I went to Shammai and I said to him, 'I will become a Jew on one condition. You must teach me your Torah while I stand on one foot.'

"Shammai thought that I was mocking him, and perhaps I was. He took the thick ruler that was in his hand and drove me away.

"Off I went to Hillel's house.

" 'Teach me your Torah while I stand on one foot,' I said to him, expecting Hillel, too, to drive me away.

"But Hillel seemed neither angry nor surprised.

" 'I will teach it to you in less time,' he said quietly. 'What is hateful to you, do not do to another. This is the whole Torah. All the rest is explanation. Go now and study it.'

"Humbly I said, 'Master teach me.' "

Of all the stories told about Hillel, this one became the favorite. People never forgot Hillel's answer, "What is hateful to you do not do to another. This is the whole Torah."

Nor did they forget his other words, "Go now, and study."

The Story of Johanan ben Zakkai

In the Shadow of the Temple

IT HAPPENED one day while Hillel was still living, that his pupils came to pay him a last visit.

"Where is little Johanan?" he asked them.

He meant Johanan ben Zakkai, the youngest of his pupils.

They looked about and found Johanan standing timidly outside the door. When they brought him in Hillel blessed him, saying, "Johanan will grow up to be great in wisdom, a teacher of many generations."

And so it was.

By the time Johanan became a rabbi he knew every word of the Torah. He knew the teachings of all the rabbis who had come before him. He also knew mathematics and astronomy and many other subjects. But his knowledge did not make him proud.

"How can one man know so much?" people would say to him.

Johanan would answer, "I learned it all from my teacher, Hillel."

Then he would smile and say, "Did you ever see an insect alight on the ocean, then rise up and shake the water from its wings? Hillel's wisdom can be compared to the ocean. My wisdom is no more than the water clinging to the insect's wing."

Rabbi Johanan's school in Jerusalem was so large that people called it the *Great House*. Yet it could not hold all who wanted to hear him. So Johanan began giving lectures out of doors in the Temple Court. He would stand before the people wearing his *t'fillin* and a long woolen *tallit* that covered his head. Its fringes reached almost to the ground. Crowds of people gathered to listen to him. The shadow cast by the Temple wall protected them from the hot sun.

In the crowd there were farmers who had lost their fields, workers who could find no work; for evil days had again come upon Judea. Cruel and greedy Roman governors ruled over the land. They taxed the people without mercy. If a man could not pay the heavy taxes, all that he owned was taken away. Leaders arose who urged the people to revolt against Rome. Among them were some of Johanan's own pupils.

Johanan, himself, was a man of peace. Once he pointed to the altar and said, "Do you know why it is written in the Torah that no iron may be used in building the altar? It is because iron is used for war. Out of iron swords and spears are made, but the altar was given us to bring peace."

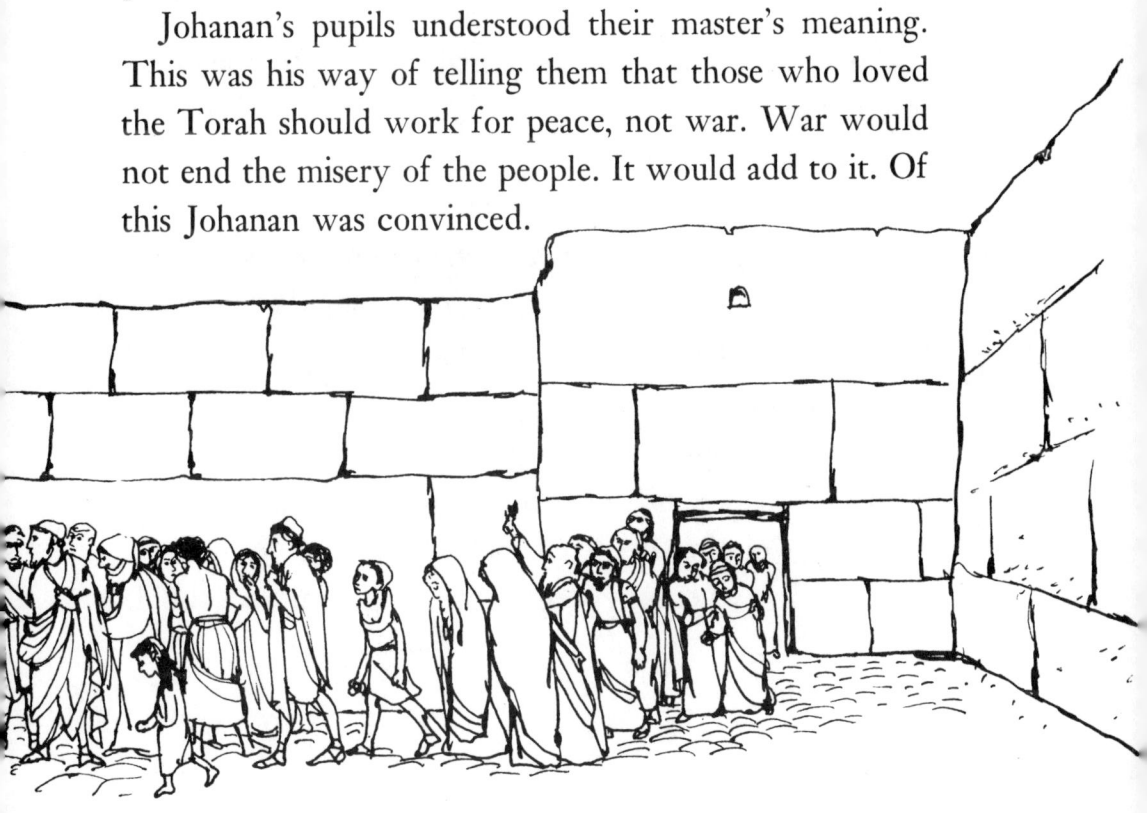

Johanan's pupils understood their master's meaning. This was his way of telling them that those who loved the Torah should work for peace, not war. War would not end the misery of the people. It would add to it. Of this Johanan was convinced.

Johanan's Pupils

Among the pupils who listened intently to Johanan's teachings were two young men, Eliezer ben Hyrcanus and Joshua ben Hananiah.

Joshua was a poor Levite, one of the singers in the Temple. People were startled when they first saw him, for he had an unusually homely face. But they quickly forgot this, as they saw the twinkle in his eye and heard his sweet voice.

More than once, Rabbi Johanan said, "Happy is the mother who gave birth to Joshua son of Hananiah."

Joshua's mother deserved the blessing, for Joshua was still a baby when she began bringing him to school.

While the learned scholars discussed important questions, she would sit in the doorway of the House of Study with the baby in her arms. She wanted the first words little Joshua heard to be words of Torah.

Eliezer was not so fortunate, though he was a rich man's son. His father was a farmer who did not believe in educating his sons. They were grown men, yet they could not read even the *Shema*. Eliezer longed to know the Torah.

One day he got up the courage to say to his father, "Father I want to leave the farm and go up to Jerusalem to study."

His father laughed at him.

"You are twenty-two years old," he said, "It is time you married and raised a family. Go back to your plowing."

But Eliezer did not go back to the plow. He left his home and went to Rabbi Johanan's school in Jerusalem.

"I have come to study Torah," he said to Johanan.

What was Johanan to do? The school was meant for grown men, not beginners. And Eliezer did not even know the *Shema*. But how could Johanan send away this serious young man who wanted so much to learn? He waited to see what would happen.

One day he noticed Eliezer pick up a clod of earth and begin chewing it. Johanan had seen people do this in a time of famine.

"The lad must be starving," he said. "His father is rich, but he ran away from home. It may be that he has no food."

"Have you eaten today?" he asked Eliezer a little later.

Eliezer kept silent.

Johanan sent for the woman in whose house Eliezer lived.

"Do you give Eliezer son of Hyrcanus his meals?" he asked.

"No," she answered, "I thought he ate with you."

"And I thought he ate with you," Rabbi Johanan said. "Between me and you we might have lost Eliezer."

After this there was no question about letting Eliezer remain in school. A young man who was willing to go hungry in order to study Torah deserved to be taught.

Rabbi Johanan saw that Eliezer was provided with food and given help with his studies. Within three years Eliezer knew as much as Johanan's brightest students.

Johanan kissed him on the forehead and said, "Eliezer is like a limestone cistern that holds the rain water. Just as a limestone cistern never loses a drop of the rain that falls into it, so Eliezer never forgets a word of Torah he has heard."

A day was soon to come when Eliezer ben Hyrcanus and Joshua ben Hananiah would help their master in the hardest hour of his life.

War With Rome

Day by day the people of Judea grew poorer. Day by day the anger against the Roman governor increased.

"Let us take arms and drive the Romans from our land," men shouted.

Johanan tried to calm the people. "We cannot win in a war against Rome," he said. "Rome has conquered half the world. It has vast armies and endless supplies. It can hold out for years."

The people answered, "King Antiochus was also mighty, but the Maccabees conquered him."

Johanan said to them, "The Maccabees were fighting for our holy laws. Rome does not interfere with our religion."

But now the Roman governor did something that the people could not forgive. One day he marched into Jerusalem with his soldiers and robbed the Temple. Part of the money which he took belonged to widows and orphans who kept their savings in the Temple. Part of it was charity money collected for the poor. The Jews looked on, helpless. Suddenly someone in the crowd began passing a basket around.

"Give charity for our governor," he cried mockingly. "The governor must be very poor to need the savings of widows and orphans." The people laughed and took up the cry, "Charity for our poor governor."

Furious at the insult, the governor ordered his soldiers to charge into the crowd. Thousand of Jews were killed on that day.

Still Johanan pleaded with the people, "Let us send a delegation to Rome. Perhaps Rome will send us a new governor."

No one listened to him. Even the rabbi who sat beside Johanan in the Sanhedrin, a grandson of the peace loving Hillel, demanded war with Rome. The pupils of Johanan were divided. Joshua, like his master, wanted peace. Eliezer was for war.

Bands of Jews armed themselves and began attacking Roman garrisons. Rome heard with amazement of the courage of this little people. It sent its greatest general

187

against them. With the general came an army of sixty thousand men, all trained fighters, veterans of many wars. They brought with them engines for hurling rocks, for battering down gates.

The Roman general landed in the north and marched down through the land, attacking every city in his way. If he could not take a city by storm, he surrounded it and starved it out. Old people, women and children fled before him. They crowded into Jerusalem, using up the stores of food.

Near Jerusalem the Roman army set up camp and waited.

"If I attack Jerusalem now, it will cost the lives of many of my men," the general said, "I will wait until the people grow weak from sickness and hunger."

Escape in a Coffin

Months passed by. In Jerusalem people were dying of hunger and sickness. Outside the city walls the Roman army waited, strong, well armed, well fed. Inside the city Jewish soldiers guarded the gates, letting no one go out lest the Romans learn of their weakness.

One day, as Johanan was walking near one of the city gates, he saw a woman stoop to pick up straws from the road.

"What will you do with the straw?" Johanan asked her.

"I will cook it to make soup for my children."

"Soup out of straw?" Johanan asked.

"It is better than soup out of nothing," the woman answered, in a dull, despairing voice.

Johanan turned to the guard at the gate, who happened to be his own nephew.

"Shall we fight on until there are no Jews left?" he said. "You know the struggle is hopeless. The city will be destroyed and with it the Temple. Let us make peace with Rome."

His nephew answered, "If I mention peace to our leaders they will kill me."

"Then help me to escape from the city," Johanan said. "I will go to the Roman general and try to save some of the teachers. If we cannot save the Temple, we must save the Torah."

That night Eliezer and Joshua were called to a secret meeting, and told of a plan that had been made. Johanan would pretend to be dead and Eliezer and Joshua were to carry him out of the city in a coffin.

Joshua protested, "Master, you are endangering your life. If our Jewish guards discover that you are alive, they will kill you. If you get through safely, the Romans may kill you."

Johanan answered, "That is a risk that I must take."

A few days later word was spread that the great master, Rabbi Johanan ben Zakkai, had died. Johanan, lying in a coffin, was carried through the streets of the city. A cloth covered his face. He scarcely dared to breathe.

At the gates, Joshua and Eliezer were stopped by the sentry.

"Who is in the coffin?"

"Our master, Rabbi Johanan ben Zakkai. We are carrying him out for burial."

The sentryman looked suspicious.

"Let me stick my spear into him to make sure."

But the second guard, who was Johanan's nephew, stopped him. Grumbling, the sentry let them pass through the gate.

Once they were out of sight, Eliezer and Joshua helped Rabbi Johanan out of the coffin, and he hurried on to the Roman camp.

Even the Roman soldiers had heard of the great Rabbi Johanan ben Zakkai. They brought him to the tent of their general.

"Hail emperor, king of Rome," Johanan said as he came before him.

The general answered impatiently, "You know that I am no emperor. The emperor is in Rome."

At that moment a soldier entered, leading a messenger who had just arrived from Rome.

The messenger bowed to the ground.

"The emperor is dead," he announced. "You have been proclaimed emperor in his place."

Amazed, the general turned to Rabbi Johanan.

"You knew this before I did. How?"

Johanan answered, "It is written in our holy books that Jerusalem will fall at the hands of a king. Jerusalem is falling. Therefore I knew you must be king."

"For this," said the new emperor, "I will grant you whatever request you make of me—provided you are not so foolish as to ask me to spare Jerusalem. Well, what is your request?"

Johanan answered, "Grant me permission to gather some of our scholars and to open a small school in the town of Yavneh."

"What a strange people the Jews are," the general thought. "This rabbi might have asked for riches and honor, and I would have given them to him. Instead he risks his life for permission to open a small school."

Aloud he said, "The request is granted."

The Roman general did not know that this little school in Yavneh was to save the people he had come to conquer.

The School That Saved a People

The new emperor went to Rome to be crowned, and his son Titus became general in his place. At once Titus began the attack on Jerusalem. Mounds of earth were thrown up around the city, and the war engines set up.

Jerusalem resisted fiercely. Small companies of Jewish soldiers would rush out of the city, and fall upon the soldiers who manned the machines. Defenders on the wall lifted the huge rocks and hurled them back with their bare hands. But the Romans brought up more and more troops. The wall was broken through at last, and Jerusalem was destroyed.

On the ninth day of Av, the saddest day in Jewish history, the second Temple like the first Temple went up in flames. Only the Western Wall was left.

The news reached Johanan in his little school in Yavneh. He tore his garments in sorrow and wept aloud. But not for long! This was no time to mourn. He had work to do.

The Jewish leaders who had led the war were now prisoners in Rome. Thousands of Jews were dead. Thousands of others were scattered in distant lands, sold as slaves. Those who remained had lost all hope.

"An end has come to our people," they cried. "The Temple is gone. The Sanhedrin is gone."

"We will set up a new Sanhedrin," Johanan said.

He gathered together seventy rabbis, the most learned of those who were left. Some of them had served in the Sanhedrin in Jerusalem. With these he opened a court in Yavneh. The scholars met out of doors in a vineyard, as they had met in the stone hall of the Temple. At their head sat a great grandson of Hillel.

The people asked, "How can we worship God when there is no Temple where we can bring our sacrifices?"

Johanan answered, "Study and prayer will take the place of the sacrifices. Morning prayers will take the place of the morning offering, afternoon prayers of the afternoon offering. On Sabbaths we will have an additional service to take the place of the *musaf*, the additional offering."

It was mid-summer when the Temple fell. As the holidays drew near the despair of the people deepened. On *Rosh Hashanah* crowds from all the surrounding towns gathered together in Yavneh. They had come to hear the *shofar* blown as they used to hear it in Jerusalem.

But *Rosh Hashanah* this year fell on a Sabbath.

Some of the rabbis said, "It is the Sabbath. We must decide whether it is permitted to blow the *shofar* outside the Temple."

Johanan looked at the anxiously waiting crowds.

"First let the *shofar* be blown," he said. "We can discuss the question later."

The old man, who had been appointed by the court, drew his long *tallit* over his head, put the *shofar* to his lips and blew a mighty blast.

"*T'kiah, Sh'varim, T'ru'ah,*" the *shofar* sounded.

The people listened, excited, stirred, shaken out of their hopelessness.

After the *shofar* blowing, the scholars said, "Now let us decide whether it is permitted to blow the *shofar* outside the Temple."

"It is too late to discuss it," Johanan said. "The *shofar* has already been blown."

Yom Kippur followed Rosh Hashanah. The people remembered how once a year, on Yom Kippur, the high priest would enter the Holy of Holies. Dressed in pure white robes, he prayed for the forgiveness of the people.

Many came to Johanan, weeping bitterly.

"How shall we gain forgiveness for our sins?" they asked. "There is no Temple. There is no Holy of Holies."

Johanan comforted them saying, "Do not weep, my children. God has given us other ways by which to gain forgiveness. Is it not written, 'For I desire mercy, and not sacrifices?' Pray, repent of your wrongdoings, do deeds of goodness and loving kindness, and God will forgive you."

Five days after Yom Kippur came the joyful festival of Sukkot. Johanan gave the people no time to mourn, but sent word to all the towns.

"Let every man take a *lulav* and *etrog* and bring them to his synagogue. Wave the *lulavim* before the Ark. Carry them in processions around the synagogue as you used to carry them around the altar in the Temple."

Each one hurried to choose a perfect *etrog*, to prepare a beautiful *lulav*, a palm branch decked with twigs of willow and myrtle. On Sukkot the people waved their palm branches before the Ark. They carried them in solemn processions around the synagogue.

"*Hoshanah*," they prayed. "Save us, O our God, save us!"

And they knew that God *would* save them. The Temple was gone, but they could still be Jews. They could still rejoice before the Lord. Rome had not destroyed them. They were a living people.

Johanan ben Zakkai's little school had saved the Jewish people.

The Story of Akiba

Akiba and Rachel

RABBI AKIBA was a poor shepherd who could not read or write. He fell in love with Rachel, his master's daughter, and Rachel loved him in return.

"I will marry you," she said, "if you promise me that you will study and become a scholar."

Akiba promised.

When Rachel's father heard that his daughter meant to marry a poor shepherd who did not know an *Aleph* from a *Bet*, he was beside himself with anger.

He said, "If you marry this ignorant man you may leave my house. I swear before God that I will no longer consider you my daughter."

Rachel married Akiba in spite of her father's anger. She went to live in her husband's little hut. Their bed was a heap of straw piled on the floor.

Akiba tried to keep his promise to Rachel. Night after night, by the smoky light of a straw fire, he bent over his slate, trying to learn the *Aleph Bet*. But it was hard to keep his mind on the letters. He was not used to studying and he had been up since dawn tending his sheep. By the time a son was born to them, he had given up trying.

The boy grew up strong and sturdy. He liked to play that he was a shepherd like his father. Rachel, watching him, would think sadly, "Is my son to be an ignorant man, the son of an ignorant man?"

Akiba guessed her thoughts. One day, as he passed a spring of water near their home, he noticed a deep groove in the rock. It had been made by the water trickling over it.

Suddenly Akiba thought, "Water is so soft, yet it has made an impression on this hard rock. Surely the Torah will make an impression even on my dull mind if I keep trying."

That very day he secured a teacher. Akiba sat on one side of the table and his little son on the other, and they studied the *Aleph Bet* together. Rachel's eyes were full of joy as she watched them. Now Akiba wondered why learning had seemed so hard. Within a few weeks he had gone far beyond his son. When Rachel saw this, she began urging her husband to go up to Yavneh to study under the great rabbis.

"Who will support you and the children?" Akiba asked; for a second child, a daughter, had been born to them.

Rachel had no answer at the moment. But a few days later she was standing near the spring where they drew their water, the same spring where Akiba had noticed the groove in the rock. The water ran down over the rock, then formed a quiet pool at its base. Rachel could see her reflection in the water. Her shawl had slipped from her head, loosening her hair. It hung down over her shoulders, long and thick and shimmering. Akiba always called it her crown of beauty.

Suddenly Rachel remembered something that a neighbor had told her that morning. A peddler was in the neighborhood, trying to buy up women's hair. He had met with little success, for in those days women did not cut their hair as they do now. Even the poorest women were unwilling to give up their long hair.

"I will sell my hair," Rachel decided. "The man will pay me well for it. Then Akiba can go to school."

She filled her water jar and hurried home. A pair of long shears were hanging on the wall, the ones Akiba used in the spring to shear the sheep's wool. Rachel took the shears down and cut off her long hair. It tumbled to the floor in a heap.

She threw a shawl over her head and hurried out to find the peddler.

It was late when Akiba returned from the fields, and the house was almost dark. The children were already asleep.

"Akiba," Rachel said, "tomorrow you may set out for Yavneh," and she shook out on the table a little sack of coins.

Akiba stared at them.

"Did you go to your father to beg for help?" he asked, distressed.

"No, no," Rachel assured him. She was as proud as he. "A peddler came buying hair—and—and I sold mine. Do not look at me so strangely, Akiba. The crown of beauty is not so important as the crown of Torah."

"What will you do when these coins are gone, my wife?" Akiba asked. "One does not become a scholar in a month or even in a year."

"I am young and strong and will find work," Rachel said. "You promised to become a scholar. Go now, and do not return until you have become one."

Akiba placed his hand on Rachel's shorn head.

"You are worthy of a golden crown," he said to her.

A few days later Akiba set out for the school in Yavneh.

The Shepherd Becomes a Scholar

At Yavneh, Akiba studied under the great rabbis who had been Johanan ben Zakkai's pupils. Among his teachers were Eliezer ben Hyrcanus and Joshua ben Hananiah. Rabbi Joshua had grown old and was poorer than ever. His home was a small hut. Its walls were blackened by soot from a charcoal fire at which he worked, for he earned his living by making needles. But his eyes still twinkled. Even the Roman rulers enjoyed his quick wit.

"No one has such ready answers as you, master," his pupils would say.

Joshua would answer, "I am not so sure. Once I met a little girl carrying a covered dish.

" 'What is in the dish?' I asked her.

"She answered, 'If my mother had wanted you to know what was in the dish, she would not have covered it'."

Then Joshua laughed heartily. He enjoyed telling a story in which the laugh was on him.

Not only did Rabbi Joshua welcome Akiba to his lectures. He arranged to have one of the younger rabbis give him special help. Akiba would listen intently to his master's words, think about them, ask questions.

One day Rabbi Joshua repeated certain statements that he had heard from his own teacher, Johanan ben Zakkai.

"I remember these statements," Joshua said to his pupils, "but I have never understood what Johanan meant by them."

"I think that I can explain them," Akiba said. And he did.

Joshua smiled in delight saying, "My pupil will be a greater scholar than his teachers."

Akiba returned home only once during his many years at school. As he drew near his house he heard women's voices inside.

"Your husband has deserted you," a neighbor was saying. "Go to the rabbis and insist that he return."

Then Akiba heard the voice of his wife Rachel, gentle but as firm as ever. "If my husband came to me this very moment, I would say to him, 'Go back to your studies and do not return until you have become a master of the Torah'."

"A second parting would be too hard," Akiba thought. "It is better that I do not see Rachel until I have become the scholar she wants me to be."

Without entering the door, he turned, and went back to school.

A Good Wife Is Rewarded

Years passed by, and still Akiba had not returned home. Nor had Rachel heard from him, for travel was difficult and messages hard to send. Then one day word came that a great rabbi accompanied by hundreds of his students was on his way to their village.

"Perhaps one of the pupils can give me news of Akiba," Rachel thought, and she joined the crowds that went out to meet the great rabbi. Her beauty had faded with the years and her hands were rough and work-worn. But her eyes, filled with longing, were more beautiful than ever.

Suddenly Rachel gave a cry of joy. She had caught sight of the great rabbi. *He was her husband, Akiba.* Rachel pressed through the crowd. The students saw a shabbily dressed woman trying to reach this master, and they pushed her aside. But Akiba stopped them.

"All that I know and all that you have learned from me, is due to this woman," he said, as he drew Rachel to him.

Then he told them that this was his beloved wife, Rachel.

That same day Rachel's father came to Akiba, not realizing that the famous rabbi was his own son-in-law.

"Rabbi," he said, "many years ago my daughter betrothed herself to an ignorant shepherd. I swore that I would never forgive her if she married him. Now I regret my hasty vow. My daughter is in need, and I long to go to her."

Akiba said to him, "When you made this vow was it because the man was poor or because he was ignorant?"

"Because he was ignorant," Rachel's father answered. "If he had known as little as one chapter of the Torah, I would have accepted him as my son-in-law."

"In that case you are free from your vow," Akiba said, "for your son-in-law is not an ignorant man but a scholar."

Then he told the bewildered old man that he was his son-in-law, Akiba.

Overcome with astonishment and joy, Rachel's father kissed Akiba's hands.

"You shall have half of all I possess," he said, "so that you may spend all your time in study."

Then he hurried to the little hut to embrace his daughter.

Rachel was now rewarded for her long years of waiting. She and her beloved husband and children lived together in comfort. A second son and a second daughter were born to them.

Akiba never tired of praising his good wife.

Once the question was asked, "Who is a truly rich man?"

One man answered, "He who owns a hundred vineyards and has a hundred servants to tend them."

Another said, "He who is content with what he has."

Akiba answered, "He who has a good wife."

Rabbi, Teacher and Judge

Akiba was now an honored member of the Sanhedrin. He served as judge, and had a school of his own. Young men were eager to study under him, and great scholars listened to him with respect. But Akiba never thought of himself with pride. It was not *he* who was important. It was the Torah.

In court, when a man was to be tried, he would say to

him, "Know before whom you are standing. Not before Akiba, son of Joseph, but before the Holy One Blessed be He."

Even now, Akiba had to leave his family for months at a time. It was one of his duties to collect charity for the poor. This meant traveling from town to town and even in distant lands. Travel was hard and dangerous in those days. But it was not his hardships that troubled Rabbi Akiba. It was what he saw as he went among the people.

Men who had once owned great estates were left with no more than a few fields. Yet they insisted on giving as much charity as they did in the good years. Even the poorest people shared what they had with others. A law had to be passed that no one was to give to charity more than a fifth of what he had.

Akiba loved the land of Israel. He loved his people. He could not bear to see them ground down by the Roman rulers. But what was to be done? Rabbi Joshua said that there were Romans who were friends of the Jews. He said that these Roman friends were trying to persuade the emperor that it was a mistake to be so harsh. Perhaps a change would come.

He must be patient. He must help the others to be patient.

A Broken Promise

It was not only their poverty, not only the heavy taxes of the Roman governors, that troubled the people. They longed for their Holy Temple. They had never given up hope that the Temple would be rebuilt.

Once Akiba with three older rabbis went up to Jerusalem to pray at the ruins. As they climbed the hill where the Temple had once stood, a fox ran out of a hole.

The older rabbis burst into tears, but Akiba smiled.

"Why do you smile?" they asked him.

"Why do you weep?" he said.

They answered, "We weep because we have seen the words of the prophet come true. 'The mountain of Zion is desolate. Foxes walk upon it'."

"I smile for the same reason," said Akiba. "Did not the prophets also say, 'The city will be rebuilt upon her ruins'? If the evil which they foretold has come to pass, the good will also come."

The rabbis said, "You have comforted us, Akiba. You have comforted us."

A day came when it seemed that the words of the prophets would be fulfilled sooner than Akiba had dared to hope. Word reached the *Sanhedrin* that the emperor was about to give the Jews permission to rebuild the Temple. People wept and laughed for joy. They forgot the cruelty of the Romans. They forgot their heavy taxes. Many of the people hurried to the ruins of the Temple and began carrying away the rubble in carts and in baskets. They said, "When permission to build comes, let the ground be ready."

But months passed, more than a year passed, and permission did not come. The people grew angry, restless.

"Why do we wait for Rome?" the young men cried. "Let us take Jerusalem from the Roman guard and build the Temple by ourselves."

Rabbi Akiba pleaded with them, "Do nothing rash. The emperor may yet keep his promise. We have waited so long. Let us be patient a little longer."

But he, himself, found it hard to be patient. Soon he would be eighty years old. His beloved Rachel had died. His first born son had died. Who knew whether he would live long enough to see the Temple rebuilt?

Then the emperor died, and a new emperor came to the throne. The new emperor was a great builder of cities and of temples. He sent word to the Jews that he was on his way to visit Jerusalem.

News of the emperor's journey passed eagerly from mouth to mouth. The emperor's ship had landed. The emperor was on his way to Jerusalem. He had visited the Temple mount. He agreed that it was wasteful to let the city remain in ruins. Jerusalem was to be rebuilt. A new Temple would arise on the site of the old.

The joy of the people knew no bounds.

Then came a last piece of news, shocking, unbelievable. *The new city was not to be a Jewish city but a Roman city. The new altar was to be a Roman altar in honor of the Roman god, Jupiter.*

A revolt against Rome could no longer be prevented, nor did Akiba try to prevent it. A leader arose from among the people, Simeon of the town of Koziba. Farmers and city men, workers and scholars, whoever could make a weapon or handle a weapon, came to Simeon's support. Many of the young men were Rabbi Akiba's students.

In a hidden valley, shut in by high mountains, the new army trained for war. To this valley came the aged Rabbi Akiba. He saw a troop of young men galloping by on horseback. Without stopping or slowing down, each one leaned over and pulled up a young oak tree with one hand. Their leader was Simeon, of Koziba, a giant of a man, fearless, daring, full of confidence and zeal.

A verse of the Bible came into Akiba's mind.

"A star (kokhba) shall arise out of Israel."

He laid his hand on Simeon's head, and blessed him saying, "Not Bar Kozibah shall you be called, but Bar Kokhba, Son of a Star."

Days of Peril

War soon broke out. Bar Kokhba's army fought with unbelievable courage. The Roman emperor sent his most experienced general to put down the rebellion. For two years Bar Kokhba held out. Never had Rome met so stubborn and determined an enemy. But the Jews were defeated in the end. A spy led the Roman troops through a secret passage into the fortress of Betar where Bar Kokhba's army was making a last stand. Not a man was left alive. Bar Kokhba fell together with his men.

The news of the defeat was still fresh, when worse news came. The emperor had determined to make an end, not only to the Jewish army, but to the Jewish religion.

"It is their religion," he said, "that gives this stubborn people their strength."

Jews were forbidden to keep any of the laws of the Torah. They were forbidden to study the Torah, or to teach it, or to appoint new rabbis. He who disobeyed the emperor's decrees was to be put to death.

On a dark night in an attic in the town of Lod, the rabbis gathered for a secret meeting. They had come together to decide a grave question: Should a man risk his life in order to teach the Torah? Should one permit young men to risk their lives to study it?

One of the rabbis said, "The important thing is to *keep* the laws of the Torah. In these dangerous times, we can do without study."

But Akiba said, "It is study that is most important. If men know and understand the laws, they will keep them. Otherwise they will *not* keep them. God showed his love for us by giving us the Torah. 'Forsake ye not my Torah,' He said to us. If we do not teach the Torah, we forsake it."

"You are right, Akiba," the others agreed. "We will keep on teaching."

His Life for the Torah

The Romans had shut down the schools. Spies kept watch on the rabbis' homes. But there were ways to fool the Romans. An old man walked along the street with a young man at his side. How were the Romans to know that the old man was teaching Torah as he went along? Young men went out into the forest carrying bows and arrows. How were the Romans to know that they were not hunters, but students on their way to secret meetings with their rabbis?

No one was watched by the Romans more closely than Rabbi Akiba. Akiba knew this. Yet he went on teaching. Each day he met with a few of his most faithful pupils, determined to teach them all that they had to know to become rabbis, judges, and teachers of the Torah.

One day a man named Pappos came to Akiba. Pappos was one of the Jews who believed that it was useless to resist Rome.

"Akiba," he said, "why do you endanger your life by teaching? You know that there are spies all around you. Are you not afraid of the Roman government?"

Akiba said to him, "I will answer you with a fable. Once a fox was walking on the banks of a stream. He looked down and saw the fish crowding together at the bottom of the water in great fear.

" 'Why are you so frightened?' asked the fox.

"The fish answered, 'Men are spreading nets in the water to catch us.'

" 'Then come up on land,' said the fox, 'and we shall live together in peace and safety.'

"The fish replied, 'Are you indeed the fox that is called the most clever of all animals? You must be the most stupid to give us such advice. If we are in danger in the water in which we were born, how much greater would be our danger on dry land?'

"The Torah is our life, Pappos," Akiba said. "What water is to the fish, Torah is to the Jew. If our people cannot live when we keep the Torah, we shall surely not be able to live without the Torah."

Not long after this Akiba was arrested. After a long imprisonment he was condemned to die by torture. Even in the moment of his death, Akiba gave his people strength. The jailors dragged him out into an open court. His flesh was torn by sharp iron combs. But no cry escaped him. His lips moved in prayer. There was a smile on his face. Amazed, the Roman governor asked, "Are you a sorcerer that you feel no pain?"

Akiba answered, "I am no sorcerer. All my life I have repeated the words, 'Thou shalt love the Lord thy God with all thy heart and all thy soul and all thy might.' Until now I have been permitted to serve God only with all my heart and all my might. I rejoice that now I may serve Him with all my soul."

With his last strength Akiba called out, "Hear, O Israel, the Lord our God, the Lord is One."

As he pronounced the word "one" he died.

Among the thousands who mourned for Akiba, were the pupils for whom he had given his life, the young scholars who were to carry on his work.

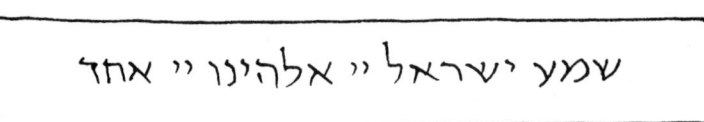

שמע ישראל יי אלהינו יי אחד

The Story of Rabbi Judah the Prince

An Exchange of Babies

PEOPLE liked to remember that Rabbi Judah the Prince was born on the day Akiba died. They said, "The sun sets and the sun rises. God took Akiba from us and he gave us Rabbi Judah."

Judah's father was Rabbi Simeon ben Gamliel, a great-grandson of Hillel. The wicked emperor had decreed that no parent was to circumcize his son. If he disobeyed the decree he was to be put to death together with the infant. In spite of this, Judah's father had the baby circumsized when he was eight days old.

The next morning there was a loud knock on the door. A messenger from the Roman governor stood outside.

"The governor commands you to bring your infant before the court," he said. "It has been reported to him that you stubborn Jews refuse to obey the emperor's decrees."

Judah's mother trembled for her baby.

Luckily not all the Romans were like the cruel rulers. Judah's mother had a good Roman neighbor who also had an infant son. The Roman mother pitied the Jewish mother.

"Let us exchange babies," she said. "Give me your Judah, and take my Antoninus before the court. The governor will think he is your son. When he sees that the child is not circumcized, he will let you go in peace."

The plan was followed and Judah's life was saved.

"May God reward you," said Judah's mother as she returned Antoninus to his mother. "May your son grow up to be a great and good man."

She did not know that Antoninus would one day become emperor of Rome, a good and wise emperor. Nor did the Roman mother know that the baby she had saved was to become one of the greatest of the rabbis.

For the Sake of the Torah

When Judah was three years old, the wicked emperor died and the cruel decrees against the Jews were withdrawn. A new school and a new court were opened, this time in the town of Usha in Galilee. Judah's father, Rabbi Simeon, became president.

It was a busy household in which the boy grew up. Important visitors came and went. There were Roman officials sent to discuss matters of government with his father. Judah understood their talk, for he had been taught to speak Greek as well as Hebrew. There were also great rabbis, judges and teachers of the Torah.

Judah's first teacher was one of the scholars whom Rabbi Akiba had taught in secret. Sometimes, in the midst of a lesson, his teacher would say, "In those days of peril—" Then Judah knew that a story was coming. The stories were not pleasant ones. Some of them, like the one about Rabbi Judah ben Baba, made Judah feel angry and sad and proud all at the same time.

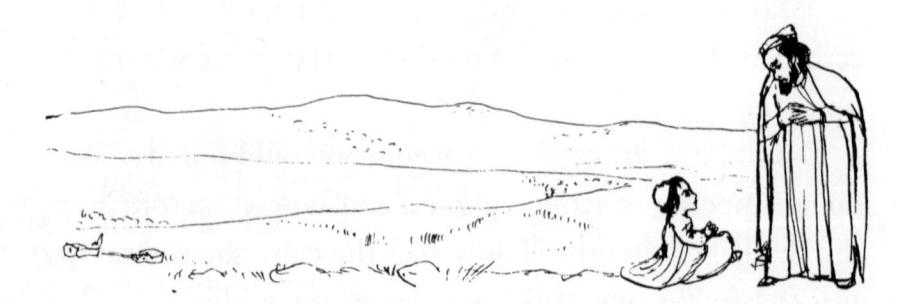

Judah ben Baba had lived in Judah's own town of Usha. It was to his home that Rabbi Akiba's pupils came after the death of their master.

" 'My children,' Judah ben Baba said to them, 'Akiba has been slain. All the pious and holy ones have been slain. And I am in my eightieth year and soon must follow them. If I do not appoint you as rabbis, there will be no one to teach the Torah.' "

"Now the wicked government had decreed that whosoever appointed a rabbi should be put to death also that the town in which the appointment was made should be destroyed. What did Judah ben Baba do? He bade the five pupils meet him in a hidden valley outside the limits of the city. There he hastily pronounced the words that made them rabbis.

"Scarcely had he finished when they heard a crackling of twigs near the entrance to the valley.

"The Romans had discovered their hiding place.

" 'Run, my children,' Rabbi Judah ben Baba said to them. 'There is a way out at the far end of the valley. You must save yourselves or there will be no one to teach the holy Torah.'

" 'Rabbi, what of you?' they asked.

"He answered, 'I will stand before the Romans as a rock that cannot be moved. Go now! I command it. For the sake of the Torah.'

"They turned and fled down the valley. Judah ben Baba stood in the narrow entrance to the valley blocking the way so that the pupils might have time to escape. In their rage the Roman soldiers pierced him with three hundred spears. When his body was found it was like a sieve."

Many times, as he grew older, Judah thought about this story.

"Suppose Judah ben Baba had not delayed the Romans," he thought. "Suppose the pupils had not escaped? Most of the laws that Rabbi Akiba gave his life to teach were not written down. Only his pupils knew them. If they had died, the laws would now be forgotten."

A question came into Judah's mind. "Why do the scholars not gather *all* the laws together and write them down? Then they would be safe even in times of danger."

Judah Becomes Judah the Prince

Very early Judah made up his mind to study under all the pupils of Rabbi Akiba.

One day Judah mounted his donkey and set forth.

He remained away from home for many years, studying now in one school, now in another. From each teacher he learned something that he had not learned from the others. In this way he came to know the entire Torah, the laws that were written down and the laws that were not written down. By the time he returned to Usha, he was ready to take his place among the young scholars of the assembly.

The elder scholars sat on benches. The young scholars sat at their feet. Judah's questions showed so much thought, and his answers were so keen, that one day one of the rabbis said, "We drink of the wisdom of this young man. Yet we let him sit at our feet."

"It is true," said the others. "Let a bench be brought and let the young man come up and sit beside us."

But Judah's father thought that his son was much too young to be given this high honor, and Judah remained among the students.

Years passed by. Judah married and became a father of two sons and a daughter. Then a year came which he was always to remember. A plague of locusts came upon the land. The locusts flew in on the wind like great dark clouds and settled upon the fields, devouring every green thing in their way. When they left, the fields were stripped and bare. In this year of the locusts Judah's father, Simeon ben Gamliel, died.

Judah mourned his father deeply. He had learned much from him—to protect the rights of servants and slaves; to see that everyone received just treatment, non-Jews as well as Jews; to seek truth and peace; to keep God's commandments joyfully.

Now Judah was to take his father's place. He was given the title of *Nasi* or Prince, and was made the head of the government, the court, and the school.

Soon after this Judah moved from Usha to the town of Bet She'arim. Bet She'arim was nearer the center of the land, convenient for the scholars of the south as well as those of the north. Here on the slopes of Mount Carmel, Rabbi Judah opened a school that became famous among Jews throughout the world. From this time he was no longer called Rabbi Judah, but simply Rabbi.

Rabbi Learns From His Pupils

Wherever Jews lived, in the Land of Israel, in Babylonia, in Rome, in Egypt, stories were told of the greatness of Rabbi Judah the Prince.

People said, "Rabbi Judah's cattle stalls are worth more than the treasure houses of the King of Persia."

This was only a story. It is true, however, that Rabbi Judah owned great estates, fields and vineyards, and rich olive groves that had come to him from his father and grandfather.

People said, "No one is so wise as Rabbi Judah. Even the Roman emperor comes to him for advice. Whenever he has a hard problem to solve, he sends for our Rabbi and they meet in secret."

This was partly true. The Romans respected Rabbi Judah and the Emperor Antoninus was his friend. He was the Antoninus whose mother had saved Judah when he was a baby.

People said, "Never have so many good things been combined in one man, riches, honor, good family, high office, knowledge of the Torah, love of God, kindness to man."

And this was altogether true.

In spite of his great wealth, Rabbi Judah lived simply, using his riches to support schools and scholars. Once, in a time of famine, he opened his storehouses and shared his grain freely with the poor.

At first he supported only scholars and their families. When ignorant folk came to ask for grain, Rabbi's servants turned them away, saying, "Rabbi's grain was not meant for such as you."

One day a young man pushed his way through the crowd that was standing about Rabbi Judah.

"Master, give me bread," he said to him.

"Are you a student of the Torah?" Rabbi asked.

The young man remained silent.

"Then why should I feed you?" Rabbi said.

The young man answered, "Feed me as you would feed a dog or a hungry raven."

"See that he is given food," Rabbi said to his servants.

When the young man had left the room, Rabbi Judah's son said to him, "Father, that young man was one of your students."

"Why did he not say so?" Rabbi asked.

His son answered, "Because he did not want to accept food that was given him only because he studied Torah."

Rabbi took to heart the lesson that his pupil had tried to teach him. From that day he opened his storehouses to all who needed help.

No Time to Sleep

No servant worked harder than Rabbi Judah. Hardly did he leave his bath in the morning, when people began coming to him—Roman officials, Jewish leaders, secretaries with letters to be answered, scholars, students with their problems.

One morning the servant was bringing Rabbi his breakfast, when the door opened. A young man looked in, hesitated, then shut the door again. Rabbi recognized the young man. His name was Levi. A few days before, Rabbi had sent him to a neighboring town to read the Torah for the people and to serve as teacher and judge.

What had brought him back so soon?

Rabbi forgot about his breakfast, and had Levi brought in.

"What has happened, Levi?" he asked.

"Trouble," Levi answered, his voice full of distress. "I alone am to blame," he added honestly. "The whole town came out to welcome me. They built a high platform and seated me on it. Then they asked me three questions of law. I could not answer them. They asked me three other questions. I could not answer them. I saw that I was really in trouble, and I arose early this morning and came to you."

"You have not yet told me the questions," Rabbi said.

Levi repeated the questions.

"You do not know the answers to these questions?" Rabbi asked wonderingly.

"Nay, I know the answers," Levi said. And he gave them all.

228

"Then why did you not answer the people as you have answered me?" Rabbi asked.

"That is what I do not understand," said the young man. "I sat on the high platform, my heart swelled with pride. Suddenly all the words of the Torah were hidden from me. I could not remember a word."

"Ah," said Rabbi, "now I understand. It was pride that caused your trouble. Go back to the town, sit before the people humbly, thinking of the Torah and not of yourself, and the words of Torah will return to your lips."

The young man thanked Rabbi and left the room, and Rabbi turned to the servant.

"Now I will have my break—"

The doorkeeper interrupted him.

"Master, there is a man who insists on seeing you. He says it is most important."

"You may bring him in," said Rabbi.

A stout, prosperous looking man entered. He had come to bring a complaint against a poor neighbor. It was the Sabbatical year, the year which comes once in seven years. The law said that in Israel in the seventh year the land was to be given a rest. No one was to plough or cultivate it.

Said the prosperous looking man, "I myself saw my neighbor tend the trees and gather the fruit." His voice sputtered with indignation.

229

"Did the man have other food?" Rabbi asked.

"No—Rabbi—but the law—"

"What would you do if *you* and your family were hungry?" Rabbi asked. "We must see to it that changes are made in this law."

He dismissed the man and turned again to his servant.

"My breakfast," he said.

Again the doorkeeper entered. He was followed by an old friend of Rabbi, one who was himself a well known rabbi and scholar.

Rabbi welcomed his friend warmly.

"Peace to you," he said. "What brings you out so early?"

"A most urgent matter," said his visitor. "I am on my way to Cesarea. (Cesarea was the city where the Roman governor lived.) The taxes on the fields are so high that the people cannot endure them. When someone complained, the tax collector said, 'Be glad that only your fields are taxed. If Rome could, it would tax the air you breathe.' Judah, you have good friends among the Romans. I thought you might give me a letter to the governor."

Rabbi answered, "Join me in breakfast. Then we will discuss the matter further."

"You may serve us now," he said to the servant. But the servant had fallen asleep while waiting for his master.

"Sweet is the sleep of the worker," said Rabbi to his visitor. "We who are busy with the needs of the community have no time to sleep."

Soft and Hard Tongues

Not only Jews in distant lands, but people who were close to Rabbi Judah told stories of his goodness and wisdom. His servant woman held an honored place in his household. He had a way of teaching a lesson that made it stick in his pupils' minds. They liked to tell of the day he invited them to a banquet at which the main course was tongue. There were hard tongues and soft tongues. The pupils ate the soft tongues and left the hard ones.

"Notice what you are doing," Rabbi said to them. "It is plain that you think a soft tongue is better than a hard one. See to it that your own tongues are soft."

A painful illness from which Rabbi Judah suffered for many years made him feel the pain of all living creatures.

Once his daughter said to him, "Father it is not fair that one so good as you should suffer in this way."

Rabbi Judah answered, "My daughter, I deserve the pain. Once a little calf on its way to be slaughtered ran to me and hid its head under my cloak. I pushed it away saying, 'It was for this that you were created.' "

"Because I felt no pity for one of God's creatures, I deserve no pity."

Sometime after this Rabbi Judah noticed his maid servant sweeping out some baby weasels that had gotten into the house.

"Do them no harm," he said to her. "Is it not written, 'God's mercies are over all his works'?"

From that day Rabbi's pain left him. His little daughter was sure it was because he had shown pity for God's creatures.

Written Laws and Oral Laws

The time had come for Rabbi Judah to begin the most important work of his life. The idea had been growing in his mind from the time he was a boy at school. He was no more than a child when he learned to recite, "Moses received the Torah on Sinai and entrusted it to Joshua, Joshua to the elders, the elders to the prophets, the prophets to Ezra and the men of the Great Synagogue." The laws and explanations Judah was now listening to, his teachers had heard from the lips of Rabbi Akiba, who had heard them from Rabbi Eliezer and Rabbi Joshua, who had heard them from Rabbi Johanan ben Zakkai, who had heard them from Hillel and Shammai. And Akiba and Eliezer and Joshua and Johanan ben Zakkai and Hillel and Shammai were only a few of the great rabbis whose teachings had been handed down.

"How precious is the Torah," Judah thought as he tried to remember these many laws. To save the Torah, Johanan ben Zakkai escaped from Jerusalem in a coffin. Rabbi Akiba gave his life to teach it to his pupils. Rabbi Judah ben Baba let the Romans pierce his body with three hundred spears so that the pupils might escape and teach the Torah to others—to *me*.

"I must remember every word of it, every law and explanation. I must remember them *correctly*."

And again he wondered why the great scholars did not gather the laws together and write them down.

Now Judah was himself a great scholar, the head of the assembly of scholars. It was for him to begin the work.

There were hundreds and hundreds of laws and teachings. Those that were written down in the Torah were called the Written Law. Those that were handed down by the rabbis were called the spoken or Oral Law.

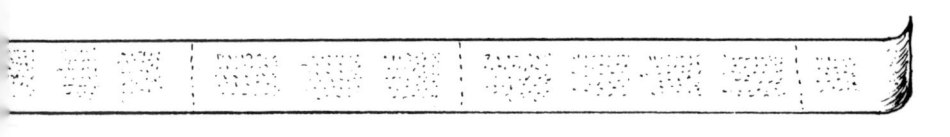

Without the Oral Law people would not have known how to keep many of the written laws.

The Torah forbade work on the Sabbath. The Oral Law explained what was meant by work.

The Torah said, "Do not plow with an ox and an ass together."

The Oral Law added, "Nor with a camel and a donkey, nor with any two animals of unequal strength."

"Why?" asked the people.

Said the rabbis, "Because the law of the Torah was given us to prevent cruelty. It is cruel to make a weaker animal keep up with a stronger one."

The Torah said, "If a man injure his neighbor, he shall pay for it—an eye for an eye, a tooth for a tooth."

Did a man whose tooth had been knocked out, knock his neighbor's tooth out in turn?

No! The Oral Law taught him better. It said, "The law of the Torah means that a man is to pay his neighbor damages for the injury."

"Should a rich man who is hurt receive more than a poor man?" the court asked.

"No," said Rabbi Akiba. "Even the poorest men in Israel are sons of Abraham, Isaac and Jacob. All must be treated alike."

Rabbi Akiba's answer also became part of the Oral Law.

This is what happened to every word and every law in the Torah. You can see how helpful it would be to the scholars and the courts if all these many laws were written down.

This was what Judah the Prince now set out to do.

The Making of the Mishnah

Rabbi Judah invited all the scholars of the land to help with the work. He wanted it to be so thorough and so correct that everyone would turn to it and follow it. He took no credit to himself.

First the rabbis gathered together all the hundreds and hundreds of laws and opinions which they had learned from their teachers. Then they decided which were most important and correct. Everyone gave his opinion.

Rabbi listened with special respect to the older scholars, but he also encouraged the young scholars to speak freely.

Once one of the rabbis said to him, "Why do you listen to these young men? It is like eating unripe grapes or drinking new wine."

Rabbi answered, "Do not look at the jar but at what is in it. There may be a new jar that is full of old wine, and an old one in which there is not even new wine."

Sometimes the scholars disagreed with Rabbi. Then he tried hard to prove his point. But he always let the majority decide.

After all the laws and opinions had been gathered together, discussed, decided upon, Rabbi divided them according to subject—laws about the Sabbath and festivals in one section, laws of marriage in another, laws that concerned farmers in a third—six divisions in all.

Then he wrote the laws down in clear and simple Hebrew, so that all might understand.

The book when completed was called the *Mishnah*. Next to the Bible, it is the most important Jewish book that has ever been written.

A Righteous Man's Monument

Rabbi began his work on the *Mishnah* in *Bet She'arim*. He completed it in a town in Galilee to which he had moved for the sake of his health. People said that the town was named Tzippori (Bird) because it was perched like a bird on a mountain top. In its clear and bracing air, Rabbi Judah spent the last years of his life. No man was more honored or loved.

When news spread among the people that Rabbi was dying, great crowds gathered about his house, weeping and praying.

Suddenly the door opened. One of Rabbi's pupils came out and said to them, "Heaven and earth were contending for the Holy Ark and Heaven won."

By this they knew that Rabbi Judah had died.

"*It is not necessary to erect monuments to righteous men. Their works are their monument.*"

This is one of the sayings of Rabbi Judah's father, Simeon ben Gamliel.

If ever you visit Israel, go up to *Bet She'arim* on the slopes of Mount Carmel. There you will find the tomb of Rabbi Judah the Prince. To see his *real* monument, go to the library of any synagogue or scholar, in any land where there are Jews, and ask for the *Mishnah*.

United Synagogue Commission on Jewish Education

Josiah Derby
CHAIRMAN

Henry R. Goldberg
VICE-CHAIRMAN

Harold Kastle
SECRETARY

Hyman Chanover
Elias Charry
Jack J. Cohen
Azriel Eisenberg
George Ende
Sylvia C. Ettenberg
Simon Greenberg
A. Hillel Henkin
Leo L. Honor
Ario S. Hyams

Philip Kieval
Alter F. Landesman
William B. Lakritz
Harry Malin
Reuben Resnik
Max J. Routtenberg
Louis L. Ruffman
Zevi Scharfstein
Abraham Simon
Samuel Sussman

Judah Goldin, *Dean, Teachers Institute, Jewish Theological Seminary*

Wolfe Kelman, *Executive Secretary, Rabbinical Assembly of America*

Abraham E. Millgram, *Educational Director, United Synagogue of America*

Bernard Segal, *Executive Director, United Synagogue of America*

Committee on Textbook Publications

Henry R. Goldberg
CHAIRMAN

Elijah Bortniker
Barnet Cohen
Josiah Derby
Morris S. Goodblatt
Solomon Grayzel

Leo L. Honor
Isidore S. Meyer
Abraham E. Millgram
Max J. Routtenberg
Saul Teplitz